# Under the Hood of .NET Memory Management

# By Chris Farrell and Nick Harrison

First published by Simple Talk Publishing November 2011

Technical Review by Paul Hennessey
Cover Image by Andy Martin
Edited by Chris Massey
Typeset & Designed by Matthew Tye & Gower Associates.

# Table of Contents

# About the authors

## Chris Farrell

Chris has over 20 years of development experience, and has spent the last seven as a .NET consultant and trainer. For the last three years, his focus has shifted to application performance assurance, and the use of tools to identify performance problems in complex .NET applications. Working with many of the world's largest corporations, he has helped development teams find and fix performance, stability, and scalability problems with an emphasis on training developers to find problems independently in the future.

In 2009, after working at Compuware as a consultant for two years, Chris joined the independent consultancy, CodeAssure UK (WWW.CODEASSURE.CO.UK) as their lead performance consultant.

Chris has also branched out into mobile app development and consultancy with Xivuh Ltd (WWW.XIVUH.COM) focusing on Apple's iOS on iPhone and iPad.

When not analyzing underperforming websites or writing iPhone apps, Chris loves to spend time with his wife and young son swimming, bike riding, and playing tennis. His dream is to encourage his son to play tennis to a standard good enough to reach a Wimbledon final, although a semi would be fine.

## Acknowledgements

I have to start by acknowledging Microsoft's masterpiece, .NET, because I believe it changed for the better how apps were written. Their development of the framework has consistently improved and enhanced the development experience ever since.

I also want to thank the countless developers, load test teams and system admins I have worked with over the last few years. Working under enormous pressure, we always got the job done, through their dedication and hard work. I learn something new from every engagement and, hopefully, pass on a lot of information in the process.

I guess it's from these engagements that I have learnt how software is actually developed and tested out in the real world. That has helped me understand the more common pitfalls and misunderstandings.

I must also acknowledge Red Gate, who are genuinely committed to educating developers in best practice and performance optimization. They have always allowed me to write freely, and have provided fantastic support and encouragement throughout this project.

I want to also thank my editor, Chris Massey. He has always been encouraging, motivating and very knowledgeable about .NET and memory management.

Finally, I want to thank my wife Gail and young son Daniel for their love, support and patience throughout the research and writing of this book.

Chris Farrell

# Nick Harrison

Nick is a software architect who has worked with the .NET framework since its original release. His interests are varied and span much of the breadth of the framework itself. On most days, you can find him trying to find a balance between his technical curiosity and his family/personal life.

# Acknowledgements

I would like to thank my family for their patience as I spent many hours researching some arcane nuances of memory management, occasionally finding contradictions to long-held beliefs, but always learning something new. I know that it was not always easy for them.

Nick Harrison

# About the Technical Reviewer

Paul Hennessey is a freelance software developer based in Bath, UK. He is an MCPD, with a B.Sc. (1st Class Hons.) and M.Sc. in Computer Science. He has a particular interest in the use of agile technologies and a domain-driven approach to web application development.

He spent most of his twenties in a doomed but highly enjoyable bid for fame and fortune in the music business. Sadly, a lot of memories from this period are a little blurred.

When he came to his senses he moved into software, and spent nine years with the leading software engineering company, Praxis, working on embedded safety-critical systems. Sadly, very few memories from this period are blurred.

He now spends his time building web applications for clients including Lloyds Banking Group, South Gloucestershire Council, and the NHS. He is also an active member of the local .NET development community.

# Introduction

Tackling .NET memory management is very much like wrestling smoke; you can see the shape of the thing, you know it's got an underlying cause but, no matter how hard you try, it's always just slipping through your fingers. Over the past year, I've been very involved in several .NET memory management projects, and one of the few things I can say for sure is that there is a lot of conflicting (or at any rate, nebulous) information available online. And even that's pretty thin on the ground.

The .NET framework is a triumph of software engineering, a complex edifice of interlocking parts, so it's no wonder concrete information is a little hard to come by. There are a few gems out there, hidden away on MSDN, articles, and personal blogs, but structured, coherent information is a rare find. This struck us as, shall we say, an oversight. For all that the framework is very good at what it does, it is not infallible, and a deeper understanding of how it works can only improve the quality of the code written by those in the know.

We'll start with the foundations: an introduction to stacks and heaps, garbage collection, boxing and unboxing, statics and passing parameters. In the next two chapters, we'll clear away some misconceptions and lay out a detailed, map of generational garbage collection, partial garbage collection, weak references – everything you need to have a solid understanding of how garbage collection really works.

Chapters 4 and 5 will be practical, covering troubleshooting advice, tips, and tricks for avoiding encountering memory issues in the first place. We'll consider such conundrums as "how big is a string," fragmentation, `yield`, lambda, and the memory management quirks which are unique to WPF, ASP.NET, and ADO.NET, to name just a few.

To really give you the guided tour, we'll finish by covering some more advanced .NET topics: parallelism, heap implementation, and the Windows memory model.

It's not conclusive, by any means – there's much, much more that could be written about, but we only have one book to fill, not an entire shelf. Consider this, instead, to be your first solid stepping stone.

Having worked with Chris and Nick before on separate projects, it was a great pleasure to find them willing and eager to author this book. With their decades of development experience and their methodical approach, they provide a clear, well-lit path into what has previously been misty and half-seen territory. Join us for the journey, and let's clear a few things up.

Chris Massey


The code examples in this book can be downloaded from
HTTP://WWW.SIMPLE-TALK.COM/REDGATEBOOKS/FARRELL_HARRISON/UNDER_THE_HOOD_IN_.NET_MANAGEMENT_CODE_EXAMPLES.ZIP

# Section 1: Introduction to .NET Memory Management

# Chapter 1: Prelude

The .NET Framework is a masterpiece of software engineering. It's so good that you can start writing code with little or no knowledge of the fundamental workings that underpin it. Difficult things like memory management are largely taken care of, allowing you to focus on the code itself and what you want it to do. "You don't have to worry about memory allocation in .NET" is a common misconception. As a result, .NET languages like C# and VB.NET are easier to learn, and many developers have successfully transferred their skills to the .NET technology stack.

The downside of this arrangement is that you develop a fantastic knowledge of language syntax and useful framework classes, but little or no understanding of the impact of what you write on performance and memory management. These "knowledge gaps" usually only catch you out at the end of a project when load testing is carried out, or the project goes live and there's a problem.

There are many thousands of applications out there written by developers with this kind of background. If you're reading this book, then you may be one of them, and so, to fill in those gaps in your knowledge, we're going to go on a journey below the surface of memory management within the .NET runtime.

You will learn how an application actually works "under the hood." When you understand the fundamentals of memory management, you will write better, faster, more efficient code, and be much better prepared when problems appear in one of your applications.

So, to make sure this goes smoothly, we're going to take it slow and build your knowledge from the ground up. Rather than give you all of the complexity at once, I am going to work towards it, starting with a simplified model and adding complexity over the next few chapters. With this approach, at the end of the book you'll be confident about all of that memory management stuff you've heard of but didn't quite understand fully.

The truth is, by the end of the book we will have covered memory management right down to the operating system level, but we will be taking it one step at a time. As the saying goes, "a journey of a thousand miles begins with a single step."

# Overview

If you think about it, an application is made up of two things: the code itself, and the data that stores the state of the application during execution. When a .NET application runs, four sections of memory (heaps) are created to be used for storage:

- **the Code Heap** stores the actual native code instructions after they have been Just in Time compiled (**JITed**)

- the **Small Object Heap** (**SOH**) stores allocated objects that are less than 85 K in size

- the **Large Object Heap** (**LOH**) stores allocated objects *greater* than 85 K (although there are some exceptions, which are covered in Chapter 2)

- finally, there's the **Process Heap**, but that's another story.

Everything on a heap has an address, and these addresses are used to track program execution and application state changes.

Applications are usually written to encapsulate code into methods and classes, so .NET has to keep track of chains of method calls as well as the data state held within each of those method calls. When a method is called, it has its own cocooned environment where any data variables it creates exist only for the lifetime of the call. A method can also get data from global/static objects, and from the parameters passed to it.

In addition, when one method calls another, the local state of the calling method (variables, parameters) has to be remembered while the method to be called executes.

Once the called method finishes, the original state of the caller needs to be restored so that it can continue executing.

To keep track of everything (and there is often quite a lot of "everything") .NET maintains a stack data structure, which it uses to track the state of an execution thread and all the method calls made.

# Stack

So the stack is used to keep track of a method's data from every other method call. When a method is called, .NET creates a container (a stack frame) that contains all of the data necessary to complete the call, including parameters, locally declared variables and the address of the line of code to execute after the method finishes. For every method call made in a call tree (i.e. one method that calls another, which calls another, and so on) stack containers are stacked on top of each other. When a method completes, its container is removed from the top of the stack and the execution returns to the next line of code within the calling method (with its own stack frame). The frame at the top of the stack is always the one used by the current executing method.

Using this simple mechanism, the state of every method is preserved in between calls to other methods, and they are all kept separate from each other.

In Listing 1.1, Method1 calls Method2, passing an int as a parameter.

```
1  void Method1()
2  {
3        Method2(12);
4        Console.WriteLine(" Goodbye");
5  }
6  void Method2(int testData)
```

```
7  {
8      int multiplier=2;
9      Console.WriteLine("Value is " + testData.ToString());
10     Method3(testData * multiplier);
11 }
12 void Method3(int data)
13 {
14     Console.WriteLine("Double " + data.ToString());
15 }
```

**Listing 1.1:** Simple method call chain.

To call `Method2`, the application thread needs first to record an execution return address which will be the next line of code after the call to `Method2`. When `Method2` has completed execution, this address is used to call the next line of code in `Method1`, which is Line 4. The return address is therefore put on the stack.

Parameters to be passed to `Method2` are also placed on the stack. Finally, we are ready to jump our execution to the code address for `Method2`.

If we put a break point on Line 13 the stack would look something like the one in Figure 1.1. Obviously this is a huge simplification, and addresses wouldn't use code line numbers for return addresses, but hopefully you get the idea.

In Figure 1.1, stack frames for Methods 1, 2, and 3 have been stacked on top of each other, and at the moment the current stack frame is `Method3`, which is the current executing method. When `Method3` completes execution, its stack frame is removed, the execution point moves to `Method2` (Line 9 in Listing 1), and execution continues.

A nice simple solution to a complex problem, but don't forget that, if your application has multiple threads, then each thread will have its own stack.

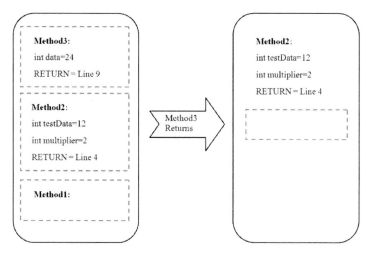

**Figure 1.1:**    Example of a stack frame.

# Heap

So where does the Data Heap come into it? Well, the stack can store variables that are the primitive data types defined by .NET. These include the following types (see HTTP://TINYURL.COM/FRAMEWORKOVERVIEW):

- Byte
- SByte
- Int16
- Int32
- Int64
- UInt16
- UInt32
- UInt64
- Single
- Double
- Boolean
- Char
- Decimal
- IntPtr
- UIntPtr
- Structs

These are primitive data types, part of the **Common Type System (CTS)** natively understood by all NET language compilers, and collectively called **Value Types**. Any of these data types or struct definitions are usually stored on the stack.

On the other hand, instances of everything you have defined, including:

- classes

- interfaces

- delegates

- strings

- instances of "object"

... are all referred to as "reference types," and are stored on the heap (the SOH or LOH, depending on their size).

When an instance of a reference type is created (usually involving the new keyword), only an **object reference** is stored on stack. The actual instance itself is created on the heap, and its address held on the stack.

Consider the following code:

```
void Method1()
{
      MyClass myObj=new MyClass();
      Console.WriteLine(myObj.Text);
}
```

**Listing 1.2:**   Code example using a reference type.

In Listing 1.2, a new instance of the class MyClass is created within the Method1 call.

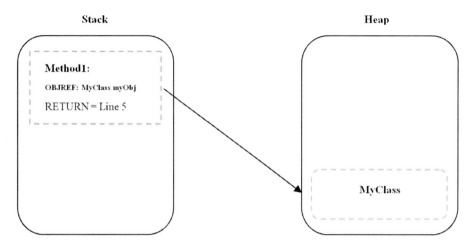

**Figure 1.2:** Object reference from stack to heap.

As we can see in Figure 1.2, to achieve this .NET has to create the object on the memory heap, determine its address on the heap (or object reference), and place that object reference within the stack frame for `Method1`. As long as `Method1` is executing, the object allocated on the heap will have a reference held on the stack. When `Method1` completes, the stack frame is removed (along with the object reference), leaving the object without a reference.

We will see later how this affects memory management and the garbage collector.

# More on value and reference types

The way in which variable assignment works differs between reference and value types. Consider the code in Listing 1.3.

```
1   void ValueTest()
2   {
3       int v1=12;
4       int v2=22;
5       v2=v1;
6       Console.Writeline(v2);
7   }
```

**Listing 1.3:** Assignment of value types.

If a breakpoint was placed at Line 6, then the stack/heap would look as shown in Figure 1.3.

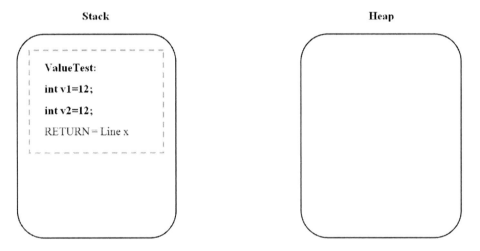

**Figure 1.3:** Stack example of value type assignment.

There are two separate integers on the stack, both with the same value.

Notice there are two stack variables, **v1** and **v2**, and all the assignment has done is assign the same value to both variables.

Let's look at a similar scenario, this time using a class I have defined, `MyClass`, which is (obviously) a reference type:

```
1   void RefTest()
2   {
3       MyClass v1=new MyClass(12);
4       MyClass v2=new MyClass(22);
5       v2=v1;
6       Console.Writeline(v2.Value);
7   }
```

**Listing 1.4:** Assignment with reference types.

Placing a break point on Line 5 in Listing 1.4 would see two `MyClass` instances allocated onto the heap.

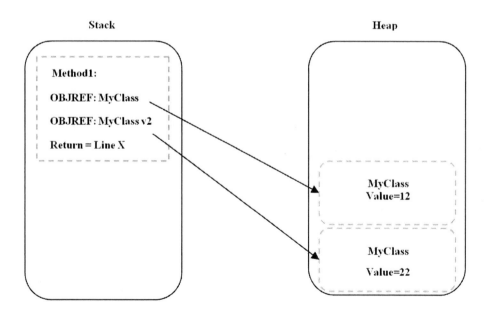

**Figure 1.4:** Variable assignment with reference types.

On the other hand, by letting execution continue, and allowing v1 to be assigned to v2, the execution at Line 6 in Listing 1.4 would show a very different heap.

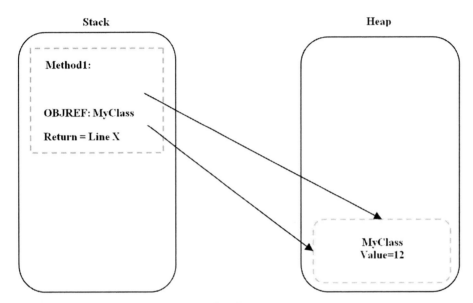

**Figure 1.5:**    Variable assignment with reference types (2).

Notice how, in Figure 1.5, both object pointers are referencing only the one class instance after the assignment. Variable assignment with reference types makes the object pointers on the stack the same, and so they both point to the same object on the heap.

# Passing parameters

When you pass a value type as a parameter, all you actually pass to the calling method is a copy of the variable. Any changes that are made to the passed variable within the method call are isolated to the method.

Having copies of value types on the stack isn't usually a problem, unless the value type is large, as can be the case with structs. While structs are value types and, as such, are also allocated onto the stack, they are also, by their nature, programmer-definable structures, and so they can get pretty large. When this is the case, and particularly if they are passed as parameters between method calls, it can be a problem for your application. Having multiple copies of the same struct created on the stack creates extra work in copying the struct each time. This might not seem like a big deal but, when magnified within a high iteration loop, it can cause a performance issue.

One way around this problem is to pass specific value types by reference. This is something you would do anyway if you wanted to allow direct changes to the value of a passed variable inside a method call.

Consider the following code:

```
void Method1()
{
    int v1=22;
    Method2(v1);
    Console.WriteLine("Method1 = " + v1.ToString());
}
void Method2(int v2)
{
    v2=12;
    Console.WriteLine("Method2 = " + v2.ToString());
}
```

**Listing 1.5:** Passing parameters by value.

Once **Method1** completes we would see the following output:

```
Method 2 = 12
Method 1 = 22
```

**Listing 1.6:** Output from a parameter passed by value.

Because parameter **v1** was passed to **Method2** by value, any changes to it within the call don't affect the original variable passed. That's why the first output line shows **v2** as being 12. The second output line demonstrates that the original variable remains unchanged.

Alternatively, by adding a **ref** instruction to both the method and the calling line, variables can be passed by reference, as in Listing 1.7.

```
void Method1()
{
    int v1=22;
    Method2(ref v1);
    Console.WriteLine("Method1 = " + v1.ToString());
}
void Method2(ref int v2)
{
    v2=12;
    Console.WriteLine("Method2 = " + v2.ToString());
}
```

**Listing 1.7:**   Passing parameters by reference.

Once **Method1** completes, we would see the output shown in Listing 1.8.

```
Method 2 = 12
Method 1 = 12
```

**Listing 1.8:**   Output from a parameter passed by reference.

Notice both outputs display "12," demonstrating that the original passed value was altered.

# Boxing and unboxing

Let's now talk about that topic you always get asked about in interviews, boxing and unboxing. It's actually really easy to grasp, and simply refers to the extra work required when your code causes a value type (e.g. `int`, `char`, etc.) to be allocated on the heap rather than the stack. As we saw earlier, allocating onto the heap requires more work, and is therefore less efficient.

The classic code example of boxing and unboxing looks something like this:

```
1  // Integer is created on the Stack
2  int stackVariable=12;
3  // Integer is created on the Heap = Boxing
4  object boxedObject= stackVariable;
5  // Unboxing
6  int unBoxed=(int)boxedObject;
```

**Listing 1.9:** Classic boxing and unboxing example.

In Listing 1.9 an integer is declared and allocated on the stack because it's a value type (Line 2). It's then assigned to a new object variable (boxed) which is a reference type (Line 4), and so a new object is allocated on the heap for the integer. Finally, the integer is unboxed from the heap and assigned to an integer stack variable (Line 6).

The bit that confuses everyone is why you would ever do this – it makes no sense.

The answer to that is that you can cause boxing of value types to occur very easily without ever being aware of it.

```
1   int i=12;
2   ArrayList lst=new ArrayList();
3   // ArrayList Add method has the following signature
4   // int Add(object value)
5   lst.Add(i); // Boxing occurs automatically
6   int p=(int)lst[0]; // Unboxing occurs
```

**Listing 1.10:** Boxing a value type.

Listing 1.10 demonstrates how boxing and unboxing can sneakily occur, and I bet you've written similar code at some point. Adding an integer (value type) to the ArrayList will cause a boxing operation to occur because, to allow the array list to be used for all types (value and reference), the `Add` method takes an object as a parameter. So, in order to add the integer to the `ArrayList`, a new object has to be allocated onto the heap.

When the integer is accessed in Line 6, a new stack variable "p" is created, and its value set to the same value as the first integer in the `ArrayList`.

In short, a lot more work is going on than is necessary, and if you were doing this in a loop with thousands of integers, then performance would be significantly slower.

# More on the Heap

Now that we've had our first look at the heap(s), let's dig a little deeper.

When a reference type is created (`class`, `delegate`, `interface`, `string`, or `object`), it's allocated onto the heap. Of the four heaps we've seen so far, .NET uses two of them to manage large objects (anything over 85 K) and small objects differently. They are known as managed heaps.

To make it the worry-free framework that it is, .NET doesn't let you allocate objects directly onto the heap like C/C++ does. Instead, it manages object allocations on your behalf, freeing you from having to de-allocate everything you create. By contrast, if a

C++ developer didn't clean up their allocated objects, then the application would just continually leak memory.

To create an object, all you need to do is use the **new** keyword; .NET will take care of creating, initializing and placing the object on the right heap, and reserving any extra memory necessary. After that you can pretty much forget about that object, because you don't have to delete it when you're finished with it.

Naturally, you can help out by setting objects to null when you've finished with them, but most of the time, when an object goes out of scope, it will be cleaned up automatically.

# Garbage collection

To achieve this automatic cleanup, .NET uses the famous (or perhaps infamous) **garbage collector (GC)**. All the GC does is look for allocated objects on the heap that aren't being referenced by anything. The most obvious source of references, as we saw earlier, is the stack. Other potential sources include:

- global/static object references

- CPU registers

- object finalization references (more later)

- Interop references (.NET objects passed to COM/API calls)

- stack references.

Collectively, these are all called root references or GC roots.

As well as root references, an object can also be referenced by other objects. Imagine the classic `Customer` class, which usually has a collection storing `Order` classes.

When an `Order` is added to the order collection, the collection itself then holds a reference to the added order. If the instance of the `Customer` class had a stack reference to it as well, it would have the following references:

- a stack-based root reference for a `Customer` containing:

    - a reference to the orders `ArrayList` collection, which contains:

        - references to `order` objects.

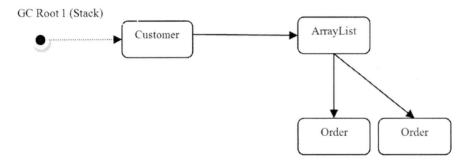

**Figure 1.6:**   Reference tree for a typical scenario.

Figure 1.6 shows the basic reference tree, with a global root reference to a `Customer` class that, in turn, holds a collection of `Order` classes.

This is important because if an object doesn't ultimately have a root reference then it can't actually be accessed by code, so it is no longer in use, and can be removed. As you can see above, a large number of objects can be maintained by just a single root reference, which is both good and bad, as we'll see later.

## Inspection and collection

To make sure objects which are no longer in use are cleared away, the GC simply gets a list of all root references and, for each one, moves along its reference tree "marking" each object found as being in use (we'll come back to what that means in just a moment). Any objects not marked as being in use, or "live," are free to be "collected" (which we'll also come back to later).

A simplified version would look something like this:

```
void Collect()
{
    List gcRoots=GetAllGCRoots();
    foreach (objectRef root in gcRoots)
    {
        Mark(root);
    }
    Cleanup();
}
```

**Listing 1.11:** Simplified GC collection in pseudo code.

The **Mark** operation adds an object to an "object still in use" list (if it's not already in there), and then iterates through all of its child object references, marking each one in turn. The result is a list of all objects currently in memory that are still in use (Listing 1.12).

Once that list is compiled, the GC can then go about cleaning up the heaps, and we'll now go through how the **Cleanup** operation works differently for both the SOH and LOH. In both cases, the result of a cleanup operation is a resetting of the "object still in use" list, ready for the next collection.

```
Void Mark(objectRef o)
{
    if (!InUseList.Exists(o))
    {
        InUseList.Add(o);
        List refs=GetAllChildReferences(o);
        foreach (objectRef childRef in refs)
        {
            Mark(childRef);
        }
    }
}
```

**Listing 1.12:** Simplified GC Mark operation in pseudo code.

# SOH cleanup – heap compaction

Garbage collection of the Small Object Heap (SOH) involves compaction. This is because the SOH is a contiguous heap where objects are allocated consecutively on top of each other. When compaction occurs, marked objects are copied over the space taken up by unmarked objects, overwriting those objects, removing any gaps, and keeping the heap contiguous; this process is known as Copy Collection. The advantage of this is that heap fragmentation (i.e. unusable memory gaps) is kept to a minimum. The main disadvantage is that compaction involves copying chunks of memory around, which requires CPU cycles and so, depending on frequency, can cause performance problems. What you gain in efficient allocation you could lose in compaction costs.

# LOH sweeping – free space tracking

The Large Object Heap (LOH) isn't compacted, and this is simply because of the time it would take to copy large objects over the top of unused ones. Instead, the LOH keeps track of free and used space, and attempts to allocate new objects into the most appropriately-sized free slots left behind by collected objects.

As a result of this, the LOH is prone to fragmentation, wherein memory gaps are left behind that can only be used if large objects (i.e. >85 KB) of a similar or smaller size to those gaps are subsequently allocated. We will look more closely at these managed heaps in Chapter 2.

It's worth pointing out that the actual algorithms used to carry out garbage collection are known only to the .NET GC team, but one thing I do know is that they will have used every optimization possible.

# Static Objects

I've already mentioned static/global objects as a source of root references, but let's now look at that topic in a bit more detail, and with some more background.

Marking a class member as static makes it a class-specific, rather than instance-specific, object. With using non-static members, you would need to declare an instance of the necessary class before you could access its members. On the other hand, static members can be accessed directly by just using the class name.

```
class Person
{
    public int Age=0;
    public static MaxAge=120;
}
```

**Listing 1.13:** Example of a static member variable.

Listing 1.13 shows both an instance variable (`Age`) and a static variable (`MaxAge`) on a `Person` class. The static variable is being used as a piece of general data across the range of `Person` instances (people aren't usual older than 120), whereas the instance variable is specific to an instance of the class, i.e. an individual person.

To access each member, you would need to write the code in Listing 1.14.

```
Person thisPerson=new Person();
thisPerson.Age=121;

if (thisPerson.Age>Person.MaxAge)
{
    // Validation Failure
}
```

**Listing 1.14:**  Accessing statics.

In Listing 1.14, an instance of a **Person** is created, and it's *only* via the instance variable that the **Age** member is accessible, whereas **MaxAge** is available as a kind of global member on the **Person** type itself.

In C#, statics are often used to define global variables.

# Static methods and fields

When you mark a method, property, variable, or event as static, the runtime creates a global instance of each one soon after the code referencing them is loaded and used.

Static members don't need to be created using the new keyword, but are accessed using the name of the class they were defined within. They are accessible by all threads in an app domain (unless they are marked with the **[ThreadStatic]** attribute, which I'll come back to in a moment), and are never garbage collected because they essentially *are* root references in themselves.

Statics are a common and enduring source of root references, and can be responsible for keeping objects loaded in memory for far longer than would otherwise be expected.

Listing 1.15 shows the declaration of a static object and its initialization within a static constructor. Once loaded, the static constructor will execute, creating a static instance of the `Customer` class, and a reference will be held to an instance of the `Customer` class for the duration of the application domain (or the thread, if the reference is marked `[ThreadStatic]`).

```
public class MyData
{
   public static Customer Client;
   public static event EventType OnOrdersAdded;
   static  MyData()
   {
       // Initialize
       Client=new Customer();
   }
}
```

**Listing 1.15:** Static reference example.

It's also worth remembering that any classes that subscribe to static events will remain in memory until the event subscription is removed, or the containing app domain finishes.

Static collections can also be a problem, as the collection itself will act as a root reference, holding all added objects in memory for the lifetime of the app domain.

## Thread Statics

Sometimes you may want to prevent multiple threads accessing a common set of statics. To do this, you can add the `[ThreadStatic]` attribute to the member, and create multiple static instances of that member – one for each isolated thread (one instance per thread), as in Listing 1.16.

```
[ThreadStatic]
public static int NumberofThreadHits=0;
```

**Listing 1.16:** Marking a member [ThreadStatic].

# Summary

OK, we've covered the basics of stacks, heaps, garbage collecting, and referencing, and how they all hang together inside the .NET framework, so we're now in a good position to delve deeper into how memory management actually works. Some of the material we've covered in this chapter has been deliberately simplified so that you get a good "in principle" understanding without being buried under the fine detail. In the next chapter, we will start looking at those finer details of how memory management works and, in particular, we'll focus on the heaps, garbage collection, and object lifetimes.

# Chapter 2: The Simple Heap Model

In Chapter 1, we saw how the stack is used to store value types and object pointers to reference types held on the heap. This enables every method called to retain the state of local variables between calls to other methods. We also touched on the heap itself, and how the creation, allocation, and destruction of objects are managed for us by the .NET runtime.

To really understand how the .NET framework manages memory for us, we need to look more closely at how heap allocation works.

## Managed Heaps

To recap, when a .NET application runs, two sections of memory are reserved for storing objects allocated during execution (we'll ignore the other two sections of the heap for now). The memory sections are called the Small Object Heap (SOH) and the Large Object Heap (LOH). No prizes for guessing the difference! The SOH is used to store objects smaller than 85 K, and the LOH for all larger objects.

## How big is an object?

I'll open this section by stating that memory is more complex than we'll be able to encapsulate in this chapter, but the picture I'll paint for you will be accurate as far as my explanations go and, more importantly, useful when it comes to helping you troubleshoot memory-related problems. It's tempting to assume an object's size on the heap includes everything it contains. In fact, it doesn't include the objects it, in turn, contains, as they are allocated separately on the heap.

Consider the following code:

```
class MyClass
{
    string Test="Hello world Wazzup!";
    byte[] data=new byte[86000];
}
```

Listing 2.1:    Allocating MyClass.

It's easy to assume that the size of MyClass when allocated includes:

- 19 characters

- 86,000 bytes.

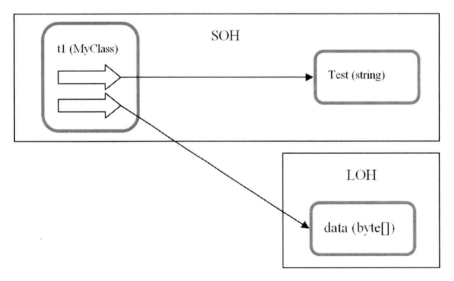

**Figure 2.1:**    Heap allocation locations.

38

In fact, the object's size will only include general class stuff, and the memory required to store the object pointers to the string and the byte array (class level variables), which are then separately allocated onto the heaps. The string will be allocated on the SOH, and its object reference held by the instance of the class; the byte array will be allocated onto the LOH, as it's bigger than 85 KB.

In Chapter 1 we discussed how object references can be held for objects which are allocated onto one of the heaps from:

- other .NET objects
- the stack
- CPU registers
- statics/globals
- the finalization queue (more later)
- unmanaged Interop objects.

To be of any use to the application, an object needs to be accessible. For that to be the case, it either needs to have a reference pointing to it directly from a root reference (stack, statics, CPU registers, finalization queue), or it needs to be referenced from an object that ultimately has a root reference itself. All I mean by that is that if, by tracking back through an object's reference hierarchy, you ultimately reach a root reference, then all of the objects in that hierarchy are fundamentally accessible (rooted).

This simple principle is the cornerstone of how .NET memory management works. Using the rule that an object which is no longer accessible can be cleaned up, automatic garbage collection becomes possible.

# What is automatic garbage collection?

Put simply, automatic garbage collection is just a bunch of code that runs periodically, looking for allocated objects that are no longer being used by the application. It frees developers from the responsibility of explicitly destroying objects they create, avoiding the problem of objects being left behind and building up as classic memory leaks.

The GC in .NET runs for both the LOH and SOH, but also works differently for both. In terms of similarities, each of the heaps can be expanded by adding segments (chunks of memory requested from the OS) when necessary. However, the GC tries to avoid this by making space where it can, clearing unused objects so that the space can be reused. This is much more efficient, and avoids expensive heap expansion.

# When does the GC run?

The GC runs on a separate thread when certain memory conditions are reached (which we'll discuss in a little while) or when the application begins to run out of memory. The developer can also explicitly force the GC to run using the following line of code:

```
GC.Collect();
```

**Listing 2.2:** Forcing the GC to collect.

Can I just add that this is never really a good idea because it can cause performance and scalability problems. If you find yourself wanting to do this, it usually means things aren't going well. My advice is: take a deep breath, then get hold of a good memory profiler and find a solution that way.

# Small Object Heap

Allocation and automatic garbage collection on the Small Object Heap (SOH) is quite a complex process. Because most of the objects allocated within an application are less than 85 K, the SOH is a pretty heavily used storage area. So, to maximize performance, various optimizations have been added which, rather unfortunately, add to the complexity.

To aid your understanding, I am going to describe the SOH at a relatively high level to start with, and then add the complexities slowly until you have the full picture. Trust me, you will thank me for it!

## Consecutive allocation on the SOH

In unmanaged C/C++ applications, objects are allocated onto the heap wherever space can be found to accommodate them. When an object is destroyed by the programmer, the space that that object used on the heap is then available to allocate other objects onto. The problem is that, over time, the heap can become fragmented, with little spaces left over that aren't usually large enough to use effectively. As a result, the heap becomes larger than necessary, as more memory segments are added so that the heap can expand to accommodate new objects.

Another problem is that whenever an allocation takes place (which is often), it can take time to find a suitable gap in memory to use.

To minimize allocation time and almost eliminate heap fragmentation, .NET allocates objects consecutively, one on top of another, and keeps track of where to allocate the next object.

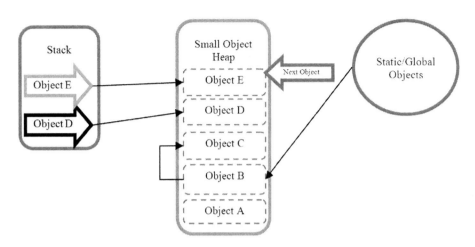

**Figure 2.2:** The Small Object Heap.

Figure 2.2 demonstrates how this works. You can see a number of objects allocated on the SOH, as well as the references that are held on the stack from other objects and from statics. In fact, all of the objects except Object A have a reference that can be traced back to a root.

Each of the objects are allocated on top of each other, and you can see there is an arrow which represents the location where the next object will be allocated; this represents what is known as the Next Object Pointer (NOP).

Because the NOP position is known, when a new object is allocated, it can be instantly added at that location without the additional overhead of looking for space in Free Space tables, as would happen in C/C++ unmanaged applications.

The only slight downside of this picture as it stands is that there is a potential for memory to become fragmented. Looking back at Figure 2.2, you can see that Object A has no references to it and it's at the bottom of the heap. As a result, it's a prime candidate to be garbage collected, as it is no longer accessible to the application, but it would leave a gap on the heap.

To overcome the fragmentation problem, the GC compacts the heap (as mentioned in the previous chapter), and thereby removes any gaps between objects. If the GC cleaned up the heap in Figure 2.2, it would look like the example in Figure 2.3 after the GC had completed its work.

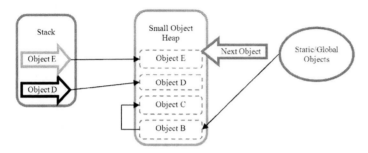

**Figure 2.3:** SOH after compaction.

Notice that Object A has been removed, and that its space has been taken up by the other objects. As a result of this process, fragmentation of the SOH is drastically reduced, although it can still happen if objects are deliberately pinned in memory (more on this in Chapter 3).

## What's still in use?

In Chapter 1 we looked conceptually at the kind of algorithms used by the GC to determine which objects are still being used and those that aren't. The rule is really very simple: "If you don't ultimately have a root reference, then you can't be accessed, so you must die." Harsh, maybe, but very effective.

When it runs, the GC gets a list of all root references and, for each one, looks at every referenced object that stems from that root, and all the objects they contain recursively. Every object found is added to a list of "in use objects." Conversely, any object not on the list is assumed to be dead and available for collection, which simply involves compacting the heap by copying live objects over the top of dead ones. The result is a compacted heap with no gaps.

Conceptually, everything I just said is correct but, as I mentioned in Chapter 1, whether the actual GC code performs "object in use" processing with a separate marking phase, sweeping phase, and compacting phase, is sometimes difficult to determine. What is clear is that the GC algorithm will be optimized to the maximum for releasing objects as soon as possible, while touching as few objects as possible. While it doesn't always get it right, that's the context you should always see it in.

# Optimizing garbage collection

If you think about it, there's potentially a bit of a problem with creating "still in use" lists and compacting the heap, especially if it's very large. Navigating through huge object graphs and copying lots of live objects over the top of dead ones is going to take a significant amount of processing time. To get maximum performance, that whole process needs to be optimized, and that's just what the .NET GC guys did.

They decided to classify all objects into one of three groups. At one end, you've got short-lived objects that are allocated, used and discarded quickly. At the other end of the spectrum, you have long-lived objects which are allocated early on and then remain in use indefinitely. Thirdly and finally, you have, you guessed it, medium-lived objects, which are somewhere in the middle.

When they analyzed typical allocation patterns they discovered that short-lived objects are far more common than long-lived ones. They also realized that the most likely contenders for GC were the most recently allocated objects. Because most objects are created within a method call and go out of scope when the method finishes, they are, by definition, short lived. So a really cool optimization was developed, which involved inspecting and collecting the most recently allocated objects more frequently than the older objects.

This was a simple and elegant approach that reduced the number of root references to be inspected and the number of object hierarchies to be navigated through. It also reduced the amount of heap compaction required.

The only slight problem lies with how they decided to name short-, medium- and long-lived objects: Generation 0 (Gen 0), Generation 1 (Gen 1), and Generation 2 (Gen 2), respectively. Obviously, they didn't consult the Marketing department first!

For all that they lack descriptive qualities, these terms are widely known and understood, and I will (only slightly begrudgingly) use them from now on, as I don't want to confuse you with my own personal preferences.

# Generational garbage collection

You know the diagram I showed you in Figure 2.2? The one that was simple to grasp, and which you clearly understood? Well, let's now throw that away (I did warn you), because we now need to think of the SOH in terms of the three generations of objects: Gen 0, Gen 1, and Gen 2.

When an object has just been created, it is classified as a Gen 0 object, which just means that it's new and hasn't yet been inspected by the GC. Gen 1 objects have been inspected by the GC once and survived, and Gen 2 objects have survived two or more such inspections (don't forget that the GC only lets an object survive if it ultimately has a root reference).

So let's look at some allocated objects in their respective generations.

In Figure 2.4, you can see each of the objects on the SOH and the generations they belong to. Object W must have survived at least two GCs, whereas Z and Y have yet to be looked at for the first time. Object X has survived one GC inspection.

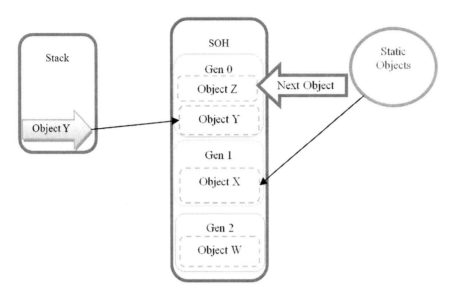

**Figure 2.4:** SOH with generations.

The GC runs automatically on a separate thread under one of the conditions below.

- When the size of objects in any generation reaches a generation-specific threshold. To be precise, when:

  - Gen 0 hits ~256 K

  - Gen 1 hits ~ 2 MB (at which point the GC collects Gen 1 and 0)

  - Gen 2 hits ~10 MB (at which point the GC collects Gen 2, 1 and 0)

- GC.Collect() is called in code

- the OS sends a low memory notification.

It's worth bearing in mind that the above thresholds are merely starting levels, because .NET modifies the levels depending on the application's behavior.

GC operation also depends on whether the application is server- or workstation-based, and on its latency mode. To avoid confusion at this stage, let's go through the general principles of generational garbage collection first, and then we will cover these more advanced topics in the next chapter.

So now let's take a look at what happens when a GC is triggered from each of the generations.

# Gen 0 collection

Gen 0 objects have never been looked at by the GC before, so they have two possible options when they are finally inspected:

- move to Gen 1 (if they have a root reference in their hierarchy)

- die and be compacted (if they are rootless and therefore no longer in use).

Either way, the result of a Gen 0 GC is an empty Gen 0, with all rooted objects in Gen 0 being copied to (and reclassified as) Gen 1, joining the other Gen 1 objects. Remember, in a Gen 0 collection, existing Gen 1 objects stay where they are.

Figure 2.5 shows the state of the SOH after a GC on the heap (as previously displayed in Figure 2.4 ). Notice how Object Y has now joined Object X in Gen 1, leaving Gen 0 empty.

Object Z didn't have a root reference, and so will be effectively overwritten by the next allocation, because the NOP is simply repositioned below its heap location.

After a GC, Gen 0 will always be empty.

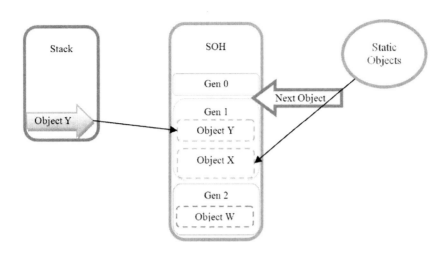

**Figure 2.5:**  SOH after a Gen 0 collection.

## Gen 1 collection

Gen 1 collections collect both Gen 1 and Gen 0 objects. Again, to illustrate, let's see the outcome of a Gen 1 collection on the heap state in Figure 2.4.

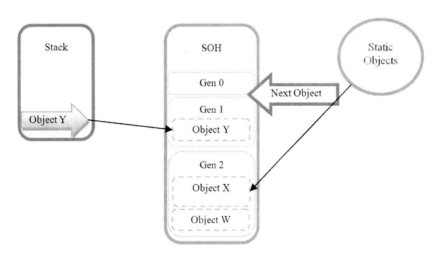

**Figure 2.6:**  SOH after Gen 1 collection.

This time, instead of Object X staying in Gen 1, it is moved to Gen 2 (after all, it's now survived two GCs). Object Y moves from Gen 0 to Gen 1 as before and Object Z is collected. Once again, Gen 0 is left empty.

## Gen 2 collection

Gen 2 collections are known as "Full" collections because all of the generations are inspected and collected. As a result, they cause the most work and are thus the most expensive.

Incidentally, if you've been worrying about why Object W has been surviving from Figure 2.4 all this time, then you can stop fretting, because it's about to die.

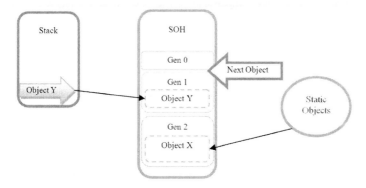

**Figure 2.7:**   SOH Gen 2 collection.

As you can see in Figure 2.7, a full Gen 2 collection results in the following:

- Object W dies and is compacted

- Object X moves to Gen 2

- Object Y moves to Gen 1

- Object Z dies and is compacted.

Obviously, the GC has had to do more work in this instance than in either of the previous collections. Ideally, you only want objects to make it to Gen 2 if they absolutely need to be there. Gen 2 is an expensive place to keep your objects, and too frequent Gen 2 collections can really hit performance.

The general rule of thumb is that there should be ten times more Gen 0 collections than Gen 1, and ten times more Gen 1 collections than Gen 2.

## Performance implications

You might be tempted to think, having learned all this, that the key to improving GC performance is creating as few objects as possible. This isn't quite right. True, the fewer objects you create, the fewer GCs you will incur; however, the key is more how many objects are removed, rather than how often the GC runs. By this I mean that, so long as your Gen 0 collections are removing a lot of objects (which is a relatively cheap process, remember), fewer objects are being promoted, and so the performance stays high.

So, in an ideal world, the vast majority of your objects should die in Gen 0, or possibly Gen 1. Objects that make it to Gen 2 should do so for a specific reason; probably because they're reusable objects that it is more efficient to create once and keep, rather than recreate each time.

If an object makes it to Gen 2, it's often (or should be) because it's actually needed. Unfortunately, you can, and will, write code where objects make it to Gen 2 only to then immediately lose their root reference. This means that they are not in use, but are potentially going to stick around and take up valuable space. In addition, if this is code that runs frequently during execution, it means that Gen 2 GC is going to happen a lot more frequently.

# Finalization

If you write classes that access unmanaged resources such as files/disks, network resources, UI elements or databases, then you have probably done the decent thing and written cleanup code in your classes to close and destroy the used resources.

Any unmanaged resource accessed from .NET won't be cleaned up by the GC and so will be left behind. If this is news to you, then please feel free to put the book down right now, go and add some destructor code to the offending classes, and we'll say no more about it.

Joking aside, if you put a destructor or a `Finalize` method (henceforth known as the **finalizer**) in your class (see Listing 2.3), then you will actually extend the lifetime of instances of your classes for longer than you expect.

You can put your cleanup code in either method below and .NET will, at some point, call it before the object is destroyed, ensuring your object cleans up just before it is destroyed.

```
class TestClass
{
      ~TestClass()
      {
      }
}

class TestClass2
{
      void Finalize()
      {
      }
}
```

**Listing 2.3 Destructor/finalizer code.**

You would probably think that, when an object is ready to be collected, and if it's got a `Finalize` method, then the GC could just call that finalizer and then compact the object out of existence. But think about it; that's potentially asking the GC to be closing files and databases and all the other stuff you might put inside a destructor (depending on your view of the theory of infinite universes, there's a finalizer out there that downloads Tom Petty's Greatest Hits and uploads them to DropBox.) What that means is that it's potentially going to slow the GC down quite a bit.

So the guys at Microsoft took a different approach, and decided to call the finalizer on objects asynchronously and on a dedicated thread. This runs periodically and calls the finalizer on all applicable objects, entirely independently of the GC.

However, that creates a new puzzle: how do you prevent an object that needs finalization from being compacted before its finalizer is called? The answer they came up with was to keep a queue of extra root references to all finalizable objects (one reference per object) and use this to keep them alive long enough to call their finalizer.

Let's look at how it works.

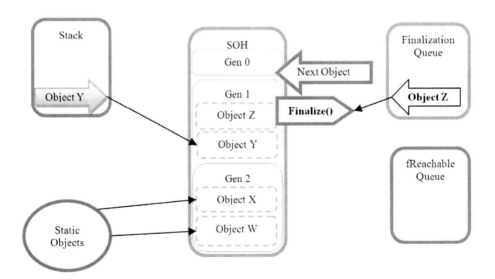

**Figure 2.8:** Finalization mechanism.

In Figure 2.8 you can see Object Z has a finalizer method on it. When it's created, as well as a root reference in one of the usual places (stack, statics, etc.), an additional reference is added onto the finalization queue, which then acts as a kind of reminder to .NET that it needs to call the finalizer on this object at some point.

When Object Z loses its root reference, it would usually become a candidate for collection but, because of the extra reference on the finalization queue, it's still viewed as "rooted," and isn't collected when the GC next runs. Instead, it's promoted to Gen 2 (assuming a Gen 1 collection occurs).

Figure 2.9 shows Object Z being promoted from Gen 1 to Gen 2, and you should notice how the finalization reference is also moved from the finalization queue to another queue, called the fReachable queue. fReachable acts as a kind of reminder list of all the objects on the heap that still need to have their finalizer called. Think of it like this; the finalization queue keeps a reference to all of the live finalizable objects and fReachable references dead objects that need their finalizer calling.

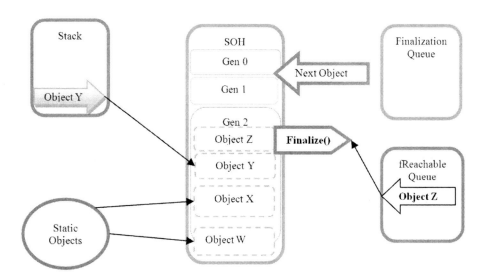

**Figure 2.9:**    Promotion of a finalizable object to a later generation.

Periodically, the finalization thread will run, and it will iterate through all objects pointed to by references in the fReachable queue, calling the `Finalize` method or destructor on each one and removing its reference from fReachable. Only then will the finalizable object be rootless and available for collection.

In the earlier example, Object Z made it to Gen 2, where it could potentially have remained for a while. What we don't know is whether Object Z was actually needed for all that time, or whether its finalization was just poorly implemented.

This doesn't mean that finalizers are bad; in fact, they are absolutely essential. But you do need to write your finalization mechanism in the right way, which is what comes next.

# Improving finalization efficiency

A simple pattern you can follow to avoid the finalization problem, is by implementing the `IDisposable` interface on your class and applying the following `Dispose` pattern:

```
public void Dispose()
{
    Cleanup(true);
    GC.SuppressFinalize(this);
}
private void Cleanup(bool disposing)
{
    if (!disposing)
{
    // Thread-specific code goes here
}

// Resource Cleanup goes here
}
public void Finalize()
{
    Cleanup(false);
```

**Listing 2.4:** Improving finalization efficiency using `Dispose`.

Listing 2.4 shows the standard **Dispose** pattern you can add to your finalizable class. All you do is provide a standard **Cleanup** method that is responsible for cleaning up the class. It needs a Boolean parameter, which is used to determine if **Cleanup** was called from the finalizer or directly from code. This is important because the finalizer is called on a separate thread, so if you are doing any thread-specific cleanup, then you need to avoid doing it if it's the finalizer running it.

Finally, we add a **Dispose** method which calls the **Cleanup** method, passing **true**. Crucially, it also calls **GC.SuppressFinalize(this)**, which deletes the reference in the finalization queue and gets around the problem.

The **Finalize** method also calls the **Cleanup** method but just passes **false**, so it can avoid executing any thread-specific code.

The developer can now use the class, and either explicitly call **Dispose**, or call it within a **using** statement (Listing 2.5). Both will ensure cleanup and avoid object lifetime extension.

```
// Explicitly calling Dispose
FinObj myFinObj=new FinObj();
myFinObj.DoSomething();
myFinObj.Dispose();

// Implicitly calling Dispose
using (FinObj myFinObj=new FinObj())
{
    myFinObj. DoSomething ();
}
```

**Listing 2.5:** Using the **Dispose** pattern to avoid object lifetime promotion.

# Large Object Heap

Thus far we've been fairly focused on the SOH, but objects larger than 85 KB are allocated onto the Large Object Heap (LOH). Unlike the SOH, objects on the LOH aren't compacted, because of the overhead of copying large chunks of memory. When a full (Gen 2) GC takes place, the address ranges of any LOH objects not in use are recorded in a "free space" allocation table. If any adjacent objects are rootless, then they are recorded as one entry within a combined address range.

In Figure 2.10 there are two free spaces that were occupied by objects that have become rootless. When the full GC ran, their address ranges were simply recorded in the Free Space table.

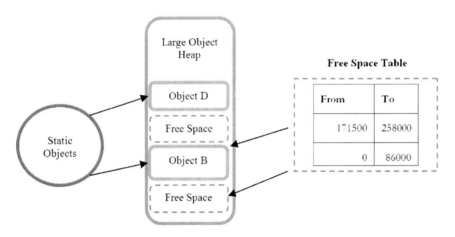

**Figure 2.10:**  LOH fragmentation.

When a new object is allocated onto the LOH, the Free Space table is checked to see if there is an address range large enough to hold the object. If there is, then an object is allocated at the start byte position and the free space entry is amended.

If there isn't (as in Figure 2.11), then the object will be allocated at the next free space above, which, in this case, is above Object D.

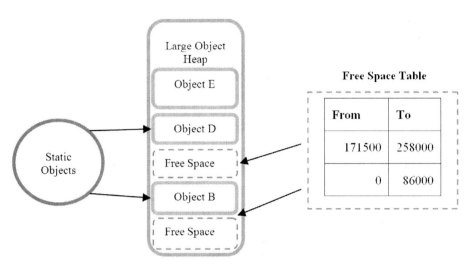

**Figure 2.11:** LOH allocation fragmentation 1.

It is very unlikely that the objects which will be allocated will be of a size that exactly matches an address range in the Free Space table. As a result, small chunks of memory will almost always be left between objects, resulting in fragmentation.

If the chunks are <85 K, they will be left with no possibility of reuse, as objects of that size obviously never make it onto the LOH. The result is that, as allocation demand increases, new segments are reserved for the LOH, even though space, albeit fragmented space, is still available.

In fact, for performance reasons, .NET preferentially allocates large objects at the end of the heap (i.e. after the last allocated object). When a large object needs to be allocated, .NET has a choice; either run a Gen 2 GC and identify free space on the LOH, or append the object to the end (which may involve extending the heap with additional segments). It tends to go for the second, easier, faster option, and avoids the full GC. This is good for performance, but it is a significant cause of memory fragmentation.

Ultimately, the memory footprint of the application becomes larger than it should be, and eventually out of memory exceptions are thrown.

Server applications are particularly vulnerable to this, as they usually have a high hit rate and, unless they use regular recycling, are around for a while.

Another reason why they are vulnerable is because, in particular, ASP.NET applications that use `ViewState` can easily generate strings larger than 85 K that go straight onto the LOH.

## You know what I said about 85 K?

I can't finish this section on the LOH without giving you the full picture. You know I said that objects >85 KB are allocated onto the LOH? Well, that works for everything except for some internal arrays, such as arrays of type `double` with a size greater than 1,000 (the threshold is different for certain types).

Normally, you would probably expect that an array of doubles would only be allocated onto the LOH when it reached an array size of about 10,600. However, for performance reasons, doubles arrays of size 999 or less allocate onto the SOH, and arrays of 1,000 or above go onto the LOH.

This makes a good quiz question if you're ever hosting a quiz for .NET developers with specialist subjects in the area of .NET memory management, or any Lord of the Rings convention. More importantly, this matters because it affects what objects cause heap fragmentation.

# Summary

From this chapter, I want you to understand the importance of object lifetime. Where and when you create an object is critical to the efficiency of your application. Adding references from one object to another, whether it's to collections, events or delegates, will likely keep your object alive for far longer than you realize. Those references will get them promoted to Gen 2 before you know it, and Gen 2 collections make your app work harder.

Don't assume that, simply because something is a local variable, it will just go out of scope. If you add a reference to it, then it could stick around for a long time, and if you do that a lot, then you could quickly end up with a memory leak or, at the very least, an application with a larger memory footprint than necessary.

I'm going to go into all of this in even more detail in the next chapter, as we build on what we've learned so far.

# Chapter 3: A Little More Detail

Now that we're starting to immerse ourselves in the inner workings of the .NET framework, in this chapter we're going to take it up another notch and build further on what's been learned so far. While we're at it, some of the simplifications made in Chapter 2 will be expanded to give you a fuller and more detailed picture.

At the end of this chapter you will have a really solid technical understanding of how .NET memory management works.

## What I Didn't Tell You Earlier

You remember the discussion about optimizing garbage collection in the last chapter? Well, I deliberately simplified it (a bit ... kind of). Let me explain what I mean.

The problem is that objects aren't always all created at the same time. Often, when objects are created, only some of their member variables are created immediately, with others only instantiating much later. This means that an object can contain references to objects from younger generations, for example, a Gen 2 object referencing a Gen 0 one.

```
class LivesInGen2forAges
{
        private SpannerInWorks _createdLater;
        public void DoABitMoreWork()
        {
                _createdLater=new SpannerInWorks();
                ….
        }
}
```

**Listing 3.1:**    Gen 2/Gen 0 reference issue example.

Listing 3.1 shows some code that could create this situation. If `DoABitMoreWork` is called once its object instance has been promoted to Gen 2, then it would immediately hold a Gen 0 reference to the `SpannerInWorks` instance via the `_createdLater` variable.

The reason this is a problem is because of the generational GC optimization I mentioned in Chapter 2, wherein the GC only collects objects residing in the generation it's collecting (and younger). As mentioned earlier, this is faster than a full collection because, as part of the collection process, the GC only needs to inspect the generations currently being collected. As a result, a Gen 0 collection won't consider object references from all of the objects in Gen 1 and Gen 2.

That's a problem because, without looking for all possible references, the GC could assume an object is no longer needed, and allow it to be collected.

Without a work-around in the earlier example, `_createdLater` would be assumed to be rootless and, with only a Gen 2 reference, would be collected in Gen 0.

.NET needs a way to detect when changes are made to object instances in later generations and the good news is that it does have a way to do this.

# The card table

A data structure called the card table is used to record when objects are created and referenced from older objects. It's specifically designed to maintain GC performance but still allow objects' references to be tracked regardless of their generation.

When Gen 0 or Gen 1 objects are created from within Gen 2 objects, the execution engine puts an entry in the card table. This check is made before any reference is created, to see if that reference is to a "previous generation" object, and is known as the "write barrier."

It's tempting to think of the card table structure as having two columns, an object reference id and a bit flag, and having one entry per object. The problem with this picture would be that the huge number of objects that need to be stored would really hit performance.

Instead, .NET stores a bit pattern, with one bit representing 128 bytes of heap memory. If an object residing within the address range of that bit has created a Gen 0 or Gen 1 object, then the bit is set.

After that, when a Gen 0 or Gen 1 collection takes place, any objects residing in the address range of a set bit in the card table are included in the "in use list" inspection, as are all of their child references.

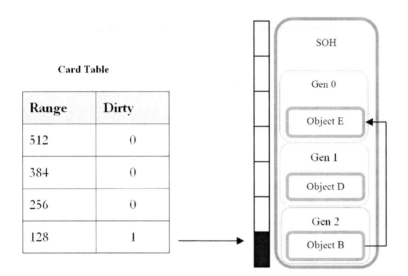

**Figure 3.1:** Simplified card table.

As we can see in Figure 3.1, Object B instantiates a reference to Object E, and marks the byte portion in the card table in which it itself resides. The next time a Gen 0 collection takes place, all child references for objects located within the pseudo example byte range 0–127 held in the flagged region of the card table will be inspected.

# A Bit About Segments

Each managed process has its own heaps for both the SOH and the LOH. Initially, at the start of a process's execution, two memory segments are requested from the OS, one for the SOH and one for the LOH.

Segments are just units of memory allocation; when the GC needs to expand the heap, it requests an additional segment. Equally, when a heap has compacted, or realizes it has excess free space, it can release segments back to the OS.

Segment size is dynamic, is tuned by the runtime, and depends on the GC mode you are running: either **Workstation** or **Server** GC. For example, a typical Workstation segment would be 16 Mb. We'll cover the differences between Server and Workstation GC later.

At the start of a process's execution, the SOH is allocated a single segment, called the ephemeral segment, to be used for Gen 0 allocations and promotions to Gen 1 and Gen 2. When it's full, a GC takes place and a new segment is added. Any surviving Gen 0 objects are copied to the new segment (becoming Gen 1 objects), and the old segment is left with just the Gen 2 objects. Figure 3.2 illustrates the process.

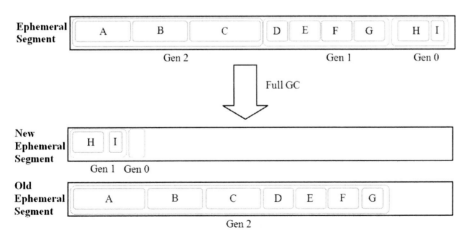

**Figure 3.2:**  The ephemeral segment (assuming all objects are rooted).

In Figure 3.2, the ephemeral segment contains rooted objects from all three generations. To prevent the diagram from getting too messy, I've not included any root references on the diagram, so let's assume all of the objects are rooted.

Over time, the ephemeral segment becomes so full that a full GC takes place, and a new segment is requested from the OS which becomes the new ephemeral segment. Objects I and H are copied to it (as they are rooted), joining Gen 1, and everything else is left behind on the old ephemeral segment. If you're thinking what I think you're thinking, you're right! Gen 2 *is* just a collection of old ephemeral segments.

## Segments and Pages

Segments are made up from virtual memory pages requested from the Virtual Memory Manager (VMM) of the OS. The VMM maps the physical memory and the disk-based page file to a single virtual addressable space, which is subdivided into pages.

Pages can be in one of three states: **free**, **committed** or **reserved**.

- **Free pages** are available to be allocated to a requesting thread.

- **Committed pages** are allocated and, ultimately, translate to pages in physical memory. As such, they can be swapped to and from the page file when necessary (paging).

- **Reserved pages** are a low overhead means of reserving virtual memory for future use, but don't translate to physical memory and don't incur paging.

Applications can either reserve pages and then commit them later when needed, or reserve and commit all at once using specific API calls.

When the GC builds a segment, it reserves the required number of pages and then commits them when needed. Redundant segments can ultimately be released back to the OS.

# Garbage Collection Performance

We've covered what happens during a GC; what with building "in use lists" and heap compaction, it's no surprise that performance can become an issue for some applications.

Take heap compaction, for example. Objects are being moved around in memory so, to ensure heap integrity, the GC has to suspend the execution of threads of the executing process. Obviously, this isn't ideal for performance, but it *is* essential to ensure that the heap is managed efficiently.

The tradeoff between performance and heap efficiency has been key to the development of a number of modes under which the GC can run. As briefly mentioned earlier, the GC has two modes: **Workstation** mode, which is tuned to give maximum UI responsiveness and **Server** mode, which is tuned to give maximum request throughput. The way the GC behaves in the two modes is very different, so I will explain them separately.

# Workstation GC mode

This mode is designed to give maximum possible responsiveness to the user, and cut down on any pauses due to GC. Ideally, you want to avoid any perception of pauses or jerkiness in interactive applications so, to achieve this responsiveness, Workstation GC mode limits the number of thread suspensions.

Since .NET Common Language Runtime (CLR) version 1.0, Workstation GC could run as either concurrent or non-concurrent; this simply refers to which thread the GC runs on. In non-concurrent mode, thread execution of the application code is suspended, and the GC then runs on the application thread. It was designed for uni-processor machines, where running threads concurrently wasn't an option.

As multicore/multiprocessor desktop machines are now very common, concurrent Workstation GC is now the norm and the default.

# Concurrent Workstation GC

Concurrent GC has a separate thread for the GC to run on, meaning that the application can continue execution while the GC runs. Crucially, object allocation onto the ephemeral segment is also allowed as the GC is executing.

It's also worth remembering that concurrent GC only applies to full GCs, so Gen 0 and Gen 1 GCs still cause thread suspension. However, instead of just suspending *all* threads for the duration of a GC, the GC aims to only suspend threads for short periods, usually twice during execution. In contrast to non-concurrent GC, which suspends all threads for the duration of the entire GC process, concurrent GC is much less prone to latency issues.

**Here's how it works.** When a full concurrent GC takes places, the start and end positions of the allocated objects on the heap are determined, and garbage collection is limited to within this "GC domain." The nice thing about this is that the application can continue to allocate objects onto the heap outside of this domain.

Figure 3.3 illustrates the process whereby the GC domain is initially determined with a start and end position, and then the GC runs (bear in mind that it doesn't show the results of the collection). We can also see that while the GC is running, the application allocates additional objects to the heap (L, M, N and O).

The application can continue to allocate objects right up until the ephemeral segment limit is reached, which is the size of the segment minus a bit of space that we will call the "No Go Zone." Once this limit is reached, application execution is suspended until the full GC is finished.

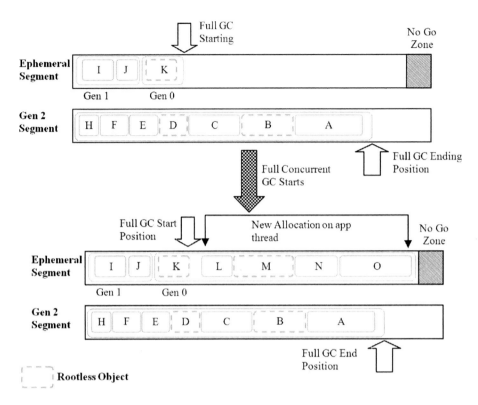

**Figure 3.3:**    Concurrent GC, which would result in the collection of objects K, D and B.

In Figure 3.3, Object M has become rootless, but it is outside of the current GC domain so its space can't be collected. It now contributes to the ephemeral segment usage even though it's no longer being used, and it's going to make thread suspension more likely to happen. That's annoying!

Ideally, we need a way of collecting garbage from both the current GC domain **and** the newly allocated objects, **and** to be able expand the heap if necessary so that thread suspension could be entirely avoided. Well, guess what those crafty Microsoft developers have done...

## Background Workstation GC mode (.NET 4.0)

You guessed it! .NET 4.0 has introduced background GC, and its aim is to do all of the above.

With background GC, a Gen 0 or Gen 1 GC can be triggered for the newly allocated objects while a full Gen 2 GC is in progress.

Gen 0 and Gen 1 now have tunable allocation thresholds which fire a background collection when exceeded, and allow rootless objects to be compacted and their space to be reclaimed. At the very least, this delays the inevitable reaching of the ephemeral segment boundary "No Go Zone."

It gets better: a background Gen 1 collection can now also create a new segment and copy Gen 0 objects into it just like in classic GC. That means there is no segment limit, which means no eventual thread suspensions due to exhaustion.

There is, of course, a price to pay for all this, and that is the fact that application and foreground GC threads are suspended while background GC executes. However, due to the speed of Gen 0 and Gen 1 collections, this is usually only a small price.

# Server GC mode

It's probably no surprise to learn that Server GC is designed to give maximum throughput, scalability and performance for server environments. It achieves this by making the GC multithreaded, with multiple threads running the GC in parallel on multiprocessors/cores.

That sounds good in theory, but how does the GC prevent all of these threads from interfering with each other? The answer is that, for each process, it allocates a separate SOH and LOH per logical processor (a processor with four cores has four logical processors).

This may seem a bit confusing until you think about what a server is typically doing, which is providing a request/response service. Request/response, by its nature, simply doesn't require state to be held on a directly shared heap; state persistence is specifically provided for as a separate mechanism. As a result, most objects created in a request/response go out of scope immediately, and so can be collected.

In this kind of scenario, maximizing the number of heaps that can be allocated to reduces allocation bottlenecks and, of course, allows garbage collection to use multiple GC threads executing on multiple processors.

On the other side of the fence, an application can certainly have threads allocating objects to multiple heaps, and there is a cross-referencing mechanism in place in the .NET framework which means that objects can still reference each other across the heaps. However, as application responsiveness isn't a direct goal of the Server GC, when Server GC runs, all application threads are suspended for the duration of the GC.

Finally, segment sizes and generation thresholds are typically much larger in Server GC (unsurprising, given the higher demands placed on those sorts of machines).

# Configuring the GC

All you need to do to configure the GC is alter your `config` file (ASP.NET applications use `aspnet.config` for your framework version). To enable Server GC, just set `gcServer="true"` in the runtime section. Obviously, for Workstation, set it to `false`.

```
<configuration>
   <runtime>
      <gcServer enabled="true | false"/>
   </runtime>
</configuration>
```

**Listing 3.2:** Configuring Server GC.

Alternatively, if you have configured Workstation GC, then you can switch on concurrency by setting the gcConcurrent enabled flag to true.

```
<configuration>
   <runtime>
      <gcConcurrent enabled="true | false"/>
   </runtime>
</configuration>
```

**Listing 3.3:** Configuring Workstation concurrency.

It's worth bearing in mind that setting the concurrency of Server GC has no effect.

# Runtime GC Latency Control

.NET Framework 3.5.1 allows the latency of the GC to be controlled programmatically, which ultimately overrides the gcConcurrent setting within your config file.

To achieve this, the System.Runtime.GCSettings.LatencyMode property can be set to one of three modes.

- **GCLatencyMode.Batch** – designed to give maximum throughput and performance for sections of an app where UI responsiveness isn't important.

- **GCLatencyMode.LowLatency** – this mode reduces the impact of GC to a minimum, which is ideal for times when things like UI responsiveness are critical, e.g. animation.

- **GCLatencyMode.Interactive** – Workstation GC with Concurrency switched on, giving a balance between GC efficiency and app responsiveness.

An obvious use of **LatencyMode** is to change it for a short period during execution of critical code that needs maximum UI or batch processing performance, and then change it back on completion.

```
using System.Runtime;
…
// Store current latency mode
GCLatencyMode mode = GCSettings.LatencyMode;
// Set low latency mode
GCSettings.LatencyMode = GCLatencyMode.LowLatency;
try
{
    // Do some critical animation work
}
finally
{
    // Restore latency mode
    GCSettings.LatencyMode = mode;
}
```

**Listing 3.4:**   Using GC `LatencyMode`.

# GC Notifications

.NET Framework 3.5.1 added notification features which allow you to determine when a full GC is about to take place, allowing you to take action if necessary. A server application, for example, could redirect requests to other servers. Basically, with NET Framework 3.5.1, you can do the following things:

- register for full GC notifications

- determine when a full GC is approaching

- determine when a full GC has finished

- unregister for full GC notifications.

In Listing 3.6 there is some example code that continually adds 1,000 bytes to an `ArrayList` in order to create increasing memory pressure, and I've added the line...

```
GC.RegisterForFullGCNotification(10, 10);
```

**Listing 3.5.**

...to indicate that I want to receive full GC notifications. The parameters are threshold values for the SOH and LOH respectively. They are values between 1 and 99, and indicate when the notification should be raised, based on the number of objects promoted to Gen 2 (for the SOH) and the number of objects allocated (for the LOH). A large value will notify you a longer time before collection takes place, and vice versa. The trick is to experiment and get these settings about right for your situation, so that you have enough time to take appropriate action.

```
System.Collections.ArrayList data = new ArrayList();
bool carryOn = true;
private void b1_Click(object sender, EventArgs e)
{
    GC.RegisterForFullGCNotification(10, 10);
    Thread t = new Thread(new ThreadStart(ChecktheGC));
    t.Start();
    while (carryOn)
    {
        data.Add(new byte[1000]);
    }
    GC.CancelFullGCNotification();
}
```

**Listing 3.6:**   Registering for full GC notification.

In my example (Listing 3.6) I am spawning a thread to monitor the GC status calling method "`ChecktheGC`" (see Listing 3.7).

In Listing 3.7 I have a `while` loop continually checking the return from `GC.WaitForFullGCApproach()`.

When it returns `GCNotificationStatus.Succeeded` I know a full GC is approaching and I can take some action, e.g. do own collection, or redirect requests, etc.

```
private void ChecktheGC()
{
 while (true) // Wait for an Approaching Full GC
 {
    GCNotificationStatus s = GC.WaitForFullGCApproach();
    if (s == GCNotificationStatus.Succeeded)
    {
       Console.WriteLine("Full GC Nears");
       break;
    }
 }
 while (true) // Wait until the Full GC has finished
 {
   GCNotificationStatus s = GC.WaitForFullGCComplete();
   if (s == GCNotificationStatus.Succeeded)
   {
     Console.WriteLine("Full GC Complete");
     break;
   }
 }
 carryOn = false;
}
```

**Listing 3.7:**    Polling for full GC notification messages.

Once the approaching GC has been detected and handled, I then wait for the full GC to take place so that I can take additional action. In this case, I may stop redirecting requests and start processing them again.

If you have a situation where garbage collection is causing you a problem, then knowing when it's about to happen may be useful to you. When and if that's the case, you may find the above pattern useful, though rather cumbersome.

# Weak References

Weak object references allow you to keep hold of objects (as they are another source of GC roots), but still allow them to be collected if the GC needs to. They are a kind of compromise between code performance and memory efficiency, in the sense that creating an object takes CPU time, but keeping it loaded takes memory. In fact, this is particularly relevant for large data structures.

You may have an application allowing the user to browse through large data structures, some of which they may never return to, but some of which they may. So what you could do is convert the strong references to the browsed data structures to weak references, and if the users *do* return to them, that's great. If not, then the GC can reclaim the memory if it needs to.

Listing 3.8 shows a contrived example of using a weak reference: loading a complex data structure, processing it, obtaining a weak reference to it for later reuse, then destroying the strong reference. Let's say that, sometime later, an attempt is made to reclaim the weak reference by attempting to obtain a strong reference from it. However, if `null` is returned from the `Target` property of a weak reference, that means the object has been collected, and so it needs to be recreated.

```
// Load a complex data structure
Complex3dDataStructure floor23=new Complex3dDataStructure();
floor23.Load("floor23.data");

… // Do some work then
// Get a weak reference to it
WeakReference weakRef=new WeakReference(floor23, false);

// Destroy the strong reference, keeping the weak reference
floor23=null;
…
// Some time later try and get a strong reference back
floor23=(Complex3dDataStructure)weakRef.Target;
// recreate if weak ref was reclaimed
if (floor23==null)
```

```
{
    floor23=new Complex3dDataStructure();
    floor23.Load("floor23.data");
}
```

**Listing 3.8:** Weak reference example.

# Under the hood

So we've seen how weak references can be used, but now we're going to take a deeper look at them. Weak references are classified as one of:

- short weak references (which ignore finalization)

- long weak references (which consider finalization).

This simply relates to how weak references work with regard to finalizable objects. If you recall from the previous chapter, finalizable objects have an extra pointer on the finalization queue that is used to keep them alive long enough for their finalizer method to be called on the finalizer thread.

Let's see how the two types of weak references differ.

## Short weak references

If you create a weak reference to a non-finalizable object or a finalizable object, but pass `false` to the `WeakReference` constructor...

```
WeakReference wr=WeakReference(floor23, false);
```

**Listing 3.9.**

...then the object reference is added to the **short weak reference table**. These references aren't considered roots, and so, when the GC runs, any references in the short weak reference table that aren't in the GC's "object in use" list are deleted.

## Long weak references

On the other hand, if you create a weak reference to a finalizable object and pass `true` to the `WeakReference` constructor...

```
WeakReference wr=WeakReference(floor23, true);
```

**Listing 3.10.**

...then the object reference is added to the **long weak reference table**. These references also aren't considered roots and, when the GC runs again, any references in the long weak reference table that aren't in either the "object in use" list or the finalization queue can be deleted.

# More on the LOH

Earlier we talked about the SOH in terms of segments and virtual memory commitment. The LOH follows the same rules and will de-commit portions of a segment that aren't being used to store live objects. This takes place during a full GC, and Figure 3.4 illustrates the process whereby Object B has become rootless and, after a full GC, is marked as free.

What actually happens is that, as mentioned in Chapter 2, the occupied memory block is marked in the Free Space table as being available for allocation. The actual pages used in virtual memory are, in fact, reset, which means that they are not paged to and from disk.

The rest of the segment, from the last live object to the end of the heap, isn't committed until needed.

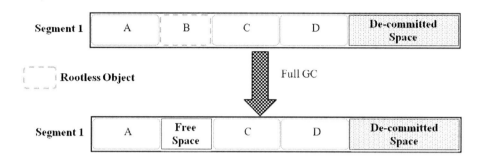

**Figure 3.4:** LOH memory model.

# Object Pinning and GC Handles

So far I have implied that the SOH is better managed than the LOH because it compacts and doesn't suffer from fragmentation issues (as mentioned in Chapter 2's *LOH* section). Well, that's not entirely true.

If you want to make calls from your .NET application to other unmanaged application APIs or COM objects, you will probably want to pass data to them. If the data you pass is allocated on the heap, then it could be moved at some point during compaction as part of GC.

This is not a problem for .NET applications, but it's a huge problem for unmanaged apps which rely on fixed locations for objects. So we need a way of fixing the memory location of the objects we pass to unmanaged calls.

# GC Handles

.NET uses a structure called GCHandle to keep track of heap objects, which can also be used to pass object references between managed and unmanaged domains. .NET maintains a table of GCHandles to achieve this. A GCHandle can be one of four types:

- **Normal** – tracks standard heap objects
- **Weak** – used to track short weak references
- **Weak Track Resurrection** – used for long weak references
- **Pinned** – used to fix an object at a specific address in memory.

# Object pinning

We can create GC Handles directly in code, and so can use them to create pinned references to objects we need to pass to unmanaged code. Listing 3.11 illustrates the use of creating a pinned handle to an object, which can then be passed to an unmanaged call.

```
byte[] buffer = new byte[512];

GCHandle h = GCHandle.Alloc(buffer, GCHandleType.Pinned);

IntPtr ptr = h.AddrOfPinnedObject();

// Call native API and pass buffer

if (h.IsAllocated) h.Free();
```

**Listing 3.11:**   Using GCHandle to pin an object in memory.

Notice how the handle is allocated using `Alloc`, and then `Free` is called once the call to the API is complete. Objects will also be pinned if you use a `fixed` block.

```
unsafe static void Main()
{
        Person p = new Person();
        p.age = 25;
        // Pin p
        fixed (int* a = &p.age)
        {
            // Do something
        }
        // p unpinned
}
```

**Listing 3.12:** Pinning using `fixed` in an unsafe block.

# Problems with object pinning

The main problem with object pinning is that it can cause SOH fragmentation. If an object is pinned during a GC then, by definition, it can't be relocated. Depending on how you use pinning, it can reduce the efficiency of compaction, leaving gaps in the heap.

The best advice is to pin for a very short time and then release, to minimize compaction issues.

# Summary

The good news is that you've made it this far, and that means you've covered a lot of fine detail about .NET memory management. We've actually got to the point where we are touching on the VMM itself, and later on in the book we will go even deeper.

In the meantime, if you want to take a deeper (but by no means definitive) look at how garbage collection works, I recommend you read through Vineet Gupta's notes on the subject. You can find them at HTTP://WWW.VINEETGUPTA.COM/2007/01/NOTES-ON-THE-CLR-GARBAGE-COLLECTOR/.

Now that you are armed with a much deeper knowledge of memory management, the next chapter will take you through the more common pitfalls and actual problems that can occur in .NET applications. Thanks to your "under the hood" knowledge, you should have a better understanding of why these problems occur, which will naturally help you when trying to fix them.

As will be explained in the next section, when you set about troubleshooting memory management problems, knowing how to fix issues is obviously essential, but tracking problems down in the first place is challenging in itself. To make life easier, it would be worth investigating memory profiling tools (such as ANTS Memory Profiler) to help you jump straight to the issues that need your attention, rather than rooting through your applications.

However you find the code that is causing memory management problems in the applications you're working on, let's now take a look at how you can fix the most common issues.

# Section 2: Troubleshooting

# What's Coming Next

In this next section of the book, we'll go on a tour of .NET and the CLR from a memory perspective. We will look at some common programming structures and idioms, and how memory comes into play as we delve into the background on some common performance issues. Chapter 4 will cover general issues and details of the .NET Framework, and in Chapter 5 we'll focus on topics specific to certain application-types, or the particular components of an application.

Clearly, there's a huge amount of ground to be covered, and while these chapters address issues that you may encounter, always bear in mind that every application is different. Although we will present general examples, individual solutions may be unique to specific application architectures. Clearly, we simply cannot cover every possible solution, but developers and architects should be able to utilize the information presented in the next few chapters to identify and fix issues in their own applications and infrastructures.

# Language

The examples presented are written in C# 4 (unless explicitly stated to be otherwise), but the information covered is true of many languages that conform to the common language specification (CLS) – the information provided here applies equally well to VB.NET. Other languages based on the .NET framework may present their own unique challenges, but they are outside of the scope for this book. Languages such as F# or Boo extend the type system, and support language features beyond the traditional .NET languages. These features are provided by the compiler as, ultimately, all .NET code is limited to the same CIL instruction set after compilation.

Of course, some languages may address some of the issues you're likely to encounter when working with C# or VB.NET more efficiently. Fascinating as this topic undoubtedly is, it's also beyond the scope of this book, and is constantly evolving, due to the growing number of available hobby languages.

# Best practices

You could spend almost unlimited amounts of time optimizing your code for better performance or memory consumption if you had nothing else to think about. However, other concerns, such as maintainability, security and productivity, *must* be considered. Often the best practice for one goal is not as applicable for another; indeed, in many cases, the opposite is true. Moreover, you might want to consider periodically profiling your application with an effective memory profiler (ANTS Memory Profiler is a good example) to ensure that your optimization efforts are targeting areas that are actually causing problems.

Ultimately, the question that you clearly need to consider is "What is the most efficient method for optimizing my code, taking these competing goals into account?" It's also worth mentioning that attempting to analyze memory can be a time-consuming task by itself, even before you've got to the stage of implementing fixes. Once again, to make your life (and troubleshooting processes) easier, it's worth investigating tools such as ANTS Memory Profiler. Assuming you've decided how best to balance your priorities, the list below outlines some sensible steps that should be taken to ensure well-behaved code in most common situations, and at minimal cost to other concerns. You may not be familiar with some of these terms or concepts now, but you will be, by the end of this section.

- Use the `IDisposable` interface with the Disposable pattern to release unmanaged resources, and suppress finalization in the Dispose method if no other finalization is required.

- Use the `using` statement to define the scope of a disposable object, unless doing so could cause an exception.

- Use `StringBuilder` when the number of string concatenations is unknown or contained within a loop.

- Initialize the capacity of a `StringBuilder` to a reasonable value, if possible.

- Use **lazy initialization** to defer the cost of instantiating members of a class if the members are not needed when the object is created.

- Use a `struct` to represent any immutable, single value whose instance size is 16 bytes or smaller and which will be infrequently boxed.

- Override the `GetHashCode` and `Equals` methods of a `struct`.

- Mark all fields in a `struct` as `readonly`.

- Use the `readonly` keyword on class fields that should be immutable.

- Implement `INotifyPropertyChanged` on component classes that may be used by binding clients.

- Avoid maintaining **large object graphs** in memory.

- Avoid using **unsigned number types** (except for byte).

- Prefer **CLS-compliant** types.

- Be aware of **variable capture** when using anonymous functions.

- Do not pass delegates to `IQueryable` extension methods.

- Avoid excessive grouping or aggregate functions in LINQ queries.

- Use **static methods** when it is unnecessary to access or mutate state.

- Initialize collections (such as `List<T>`) with the target size, if it is known.

- Consider using content instead of embedded resources for larger artifacts.

- In an IIS hosted application, set the `//compilation/system.web/compilation/debug` attribute to `false` before releasing to production.

- Remove event handlers before disposing of an object.

## Symptom flowcharts

The following flowcharts may help guide you to relevant sections, based on the specific issues you are seeing, which will help to apply the information we're going to cover.

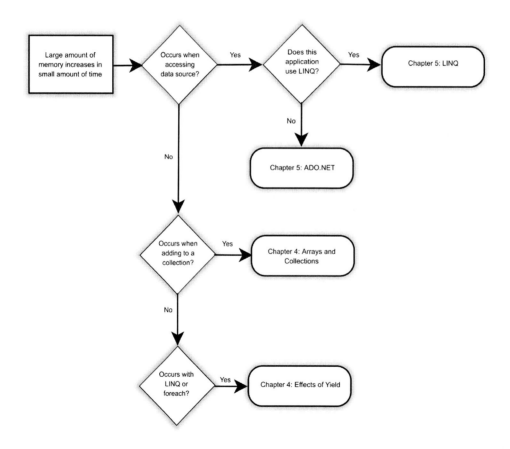

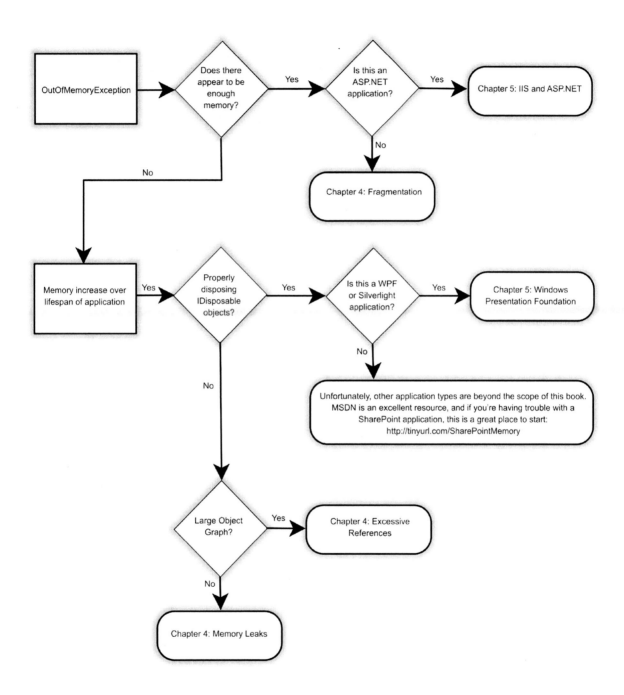

OutOfMemoryException

Does there appear to be enough memory?

Yes → Is this an ASP.NET application?

Yes → Chapter 5: IIS and ASP.NET

No → Chapter 4: Fragmentation

No → Memory increase over lifespan of application

Yes → Properly disposing IDisposable objects?

Yes → Is this a WPF or Silverlight application?

Yes → Chapter 5: Windows Presentation Foundation

No → Unfortunately, other application types are beyond the scope of this book. MSDN is an excellent resource, and if you're having trouble with a SharePoint application, this is a great place to start: http://tinyurl.com/SharePointMemory

No → Large Object Graph?

Yes → Chapter 4: Excessive References

No → Chapter 4: Memory Leaks

# Chapter 4: Common Memory Problems

The .NET Framework is, quite simply, huge, with many areas affecting memory management and potentially causing memory problems, some of which we'll explore in this chapter. We will start by reviewing the basic type system and how this affects memory usage. We will then take a deep dive into the `Dispose` pattern, exploring how this will impact memory usage and the way the GC (GC) performs.

Along the way, we will also find some surprising things affecting memory. The .NET Framework does a lot for us and some of this adds extra overhead that we easily forget about. How do immutable strings affect memory? What about the overhead of a class header? We will explore these, and other questions, as we consider the differences between classes and structs, and explore the size of an object.

The latest framework version also introduces some new concepts that, while exciting, also present new challenges and potential benefits for memory management. Most of us probably never give a second thought to how a lambda expression affects memory, and the `yield` statement is arguably the least understood keyword added to the language.

Finally, we will explore how some programming styles can affect memory, complicating the GC's job. We will see how excessive references, excessive writes, and long-lived objects can all lead to fragmentation, and make it harder for the GC to function successfully.

This may sound like a daunting journey, but when we are through you will be much better attuned to how your choices affect memory.

# Types

The type system in .NET consists of **value** and **reference** types: a value type is a **primitive** or **struct**, and a reference type is a **pointer**. In practical terms, while a value type will simply represent the current value for whatever variable you are dealing with, reference types are a bit more complicated. There are two components to the data in a reference type, specifically, the **reference** and the actual **data**. The reference is stored in the stack, and it contains the memory location (in the heap) where the data is actually stored.

A type itself describes the possible data that it can hold, along with the operations it can perform on that data. Every variable has a type that fully describes it, and it may also have types that provide a partial description, such as an interface.

```
DateTime valueType = DateTime.Now;
IComparable partialDescription = valueType;
List<string> referenceType = new List<string>();
IEnumerable<string> partialDescription2 = referenceType;
```

**Listing 4.1:** Switching from the type to an interface.

In this example, `valueType` is a `DateTime` and so can do anything that a `DateTime` can do, but `partialDescription` is an `IComparable` and can only do what an `IComparable` can do, even though both variables have the same data and refer to the same location in memory.

Let's take a look at these two main .NET types, and see how their nature and operations can give rise to bugs and memory leaks.

# Value types

Value types consist of **simple** types, **enum** types, **struct** types, and **nullable types.** Value types do not support user-defined inheritance, but they do have an inheritance chain as follows:

- Enums inherit from `System.Enum`, which inherits from `System.ValueType`

- nullable types are structs, and structs inherit from `System.ValueType`, which inherits from `System.Object`.

Variables of these types maintain their own copies of their data so, when a value is assigned from one variable to another, the data stored in the memory at one location (i.e. the memory allocated to the initial variable) is copied into the memory allocated for the new variable.

```
int x = 8;
int y = x;
Assert.AreEqual(y, 8);
Assert.AreNotSame(x, y);
```

**Listing 4.2:**  Even if value types have the same value they may, in fact, refer to different locations.

The values may be equal, but modifying the value of **y** (e.g. with the ++ operator) will not affect the **x** variable. This is often the source of bugs when developers forget that changes to a value type parameter will not carry over to the calling method.

The exception to the *One variable, one memory location* rule is usage of the `ref` and `out` keywords, which we can see in Listing 4.3.

```
private void Increment(int value)
 {
  value++;
 }

private void Increment(ref int value)
 {
  value++;
 }

private void IncrementOut(out int value)
 {
  value = default(int);
  value++;
 }

[TestMethod]
public void OutRefTest()
 {
  int x = 7;
  Increment(x);
  Assert.AreEqual(7, x);
  Increment(ref x);
  Assert.AreEqual(8, x);
  IncrementOut(out x);
  Assert.AreEqual(1, x);
 }
```

**Listing 4.3:** The effects of out and ref parameters.

The first Increment(x) call copies the value into the parameter for the method and, as the value is never returned, the variable x remains the same. The second call is to the ref version of Increment.

The ref keyword allows a value to be passed in, modified, and then passed out. This method call works as desired and increments the number. Calling the ref function with an initialized variable will result in a compile-time error.

The out parameter is another source of confusion for many. It works like the ref keyword in that it passes the value out, but the value for the incoming parameter is not copied. The parameter for the method does not need to be initialized before the call, but it must be initialized within the body of the method. This causes the `IncrementOut` method to always return 1. Calling the `out` function with an initialized variable will cause that value to be discarded.

# Reference types

Reference types include **class** types, **interface** types, **array** types, and **delegate** types. They differ from value types in that reference types store references to their values, and require memory allocation on the managed heap. Individual variables can reference the same value or object, and perform operations that affect other variables that have the same reference.

```
var person = new Person { FirstName = "Thomas", LastName = "Jefferson" };
var other = person;
person.LastName = "Paine";
Assert.AreEqual("Paine", other.LastName);
```

**Listing 4.4:** Two reference values can refer to the same memory location.

In this previous example, the only thing copied during the assignment statement was the reference – the `person` and `other` variables both refer to the same memory location on the heap.

## Boxing and unboxing

Value types can be converted to reference types through a process known as **boxing**, and back into value types through **unboxing**. In C#, this is as simple as casting the value type to a corresponding base type: `System.Enum` for enum types, and both `System.ValueType` and `System.Object` work for all value types. Boxed `nullable` types will have a null reference if the HasValue property is false, and will otherwise perform a bitwise copy of its Value property.

```
int x = 8;
// Box
object y = (object)x;
// Unbox
int z = (int)y;
```

**Listing 4.5:**   A simple case of boxing and unboxing.

Boxing is sometimes necessary, but it should be avoided if at all possible, because it will slow down performance and increase memory requirements. For example, when a value type is boxed, a new reference type is created and the value is copied from the value type to the newly created reference type; this takes time and extra memory (a little bit more than twice the memory of the original value type).

Boxing can be avoided by using parameterized classes and methods, which is implemented using generics; in fact this was the *motivation* for adding generics.

```
public void BoxedCall(object value)
{
  // Perform operation on value
}

public void NonboxedCall<T>(T value)
{
  // Perform operation on value
}
```

**Listing 4.6:**   A method signature that may require boxing and one that would not.

Calls to the BoxedCall method will perform a boxing operation on value types, and calls to the NonboxedCall method will not. With generic inference, the type can be determined at compile time. This will improve the performance of code and will also prevent the creation of an object on the heap to be collected.

```
int x = 7;
BoxedCall(x);
NonboxedCall(x);
```

**Listing 4.7:** Calling the two methods on a simple value type.

The type parameter for the call to `NonboxedCall` is inferred based on its usage. It could also have been written as in Listing 4.8.

```
int x = 7;
BoxedCall(x);
NonboxedCall<int>(x);
```

**Listing 4.8:** Calling the two methods on a simple value type without generic type inference.

As long as the compiler can infer the type parameter, leave it out. Specifying it in such cases does not add any clarity and will often create confusion.

# Memory Leaks

Memory leaks occur when accessing unmanaged code that does not properly manage its memory. As discussed in previous chapters, dead objects in managed code are handled by the GC. Dead objects are automatically collected. While behavior that looks suspiciously like memory leaks *can* occur in managed code, the cause is subtly (but importantly) different, and we'll briefly touch upon the distinction in a moment. Thanks to the GC, a true memory leak is rare in managed code.

Unmanaged resources should be released when they are no longer needed, and the onus to do this is, naturally, entirely on the developer. In stamping out memory leaks, you will spend a good deal of time working through your code handling these situations to ensure that your application is properly releasing references to any expensive unmanaged (or "system") resources.

Pseudo memory leaks (memory hogs) occur when the GC is unable to collect objects because they are being kept alive by other objects. This is a coding error and can be fixed by analyzing the code which references the object in question. Although not a true memory leak (as the developer is not directly responsible for resource allocation), the effect is the same: the application consumes more resources than necessary and, in worst case scenarios, encounters out of memory exceptions. With proper attention paid to the object lifespan, this can be avoided even in long-running applications. We will explore various issues that cause such memory leaks throughout the rest of this chapter.

# Disposing of unmanaged resources

The `IDisposable` interface defines the `Dispose` method used to release allocated (i.e. unmanaged) resources. When utilizing a class that implements this interface, it is clearly best to ensure that the `Dispose` method is called when the object is no longer needed. There are two ways to do so without an exception preventing the method's execution.

```
FileStream stream = new FileStream("message.txt", FileMode.Open);
try
{
 StreamReader reader = new StreamReader(stream);
 try
 {
   Console.WriteLine(reader.ReadToEnd());
 }
 finally
 {
   reader.Dispose();
 }
}
finally
{
 stream.Dispose();
}
```

**Listing 4.9:** Calling the `Dispose` method through a `finally` block.

```
using (FileStream stream = new FileStream("message.txt", FileMode.Open))
using (StreamReader reader = new StreamReader(stream))
{
 Console.WriteLine(reader.ReadToEnd());
}
```

**Listing 4.10:** Calling the `Dispose` method with a `using` statement.

In most situations, the `using` syntax is cleaner, but there will be times when a `try` block is preferable. Later, we will see an example in WCF where the `Disposable` pattern is not implemented properly, causing an exception to be thrown and the `Dispose` method to be ignored. In this case, we want to use the `finally` statement to ensure that the `Dispose` will be called even if there is an exception.

The important thing is that the `Dispose` method is called, whether explicitly or implicitly. If it is not, and the `Disposable` pattern is implemented properly in the object, its resources will still be picked up at garbage collection. But this will be done in a non-deterministic way, since we don't know when the GC will run. More importantly, the process of garbage collection is complicated enough without having to worry about disposing of our objects, and having to dispose of our managed resources will slow this process down.

So, as a best practice, if an object implements the `IDisposable` interface, call the `Dispose` method when you're finished with it, employing either a `using` statement or the `finalize` block. Either approach will result in the resources being freed in a more timely manner and will simplify the garbage collection process.

# Finalization

A common problem with custom implementations of disposable objects is that these implementations are not complete, and so resources are not released. This is the definition of the IDisposable interface (see Figure 4.1) and this is sometimes directly implemented on a class without any attention given to the finalizer (if you are tempted to draw parallels to destructors, don't. They are syntactically similar, but semantically very different).

**Figure 4.1:**   The IDisposable definition.

```
public class Sample :IDisposable
{
  public void Dispose()
  {
    // Clean up resources
  }
}
```

**Listing 4.11:**  Sample implementation of the interface.

The issue arises when the Dispose method isn't called. Despite all the best practices, it is important to realize that not everyone remembers to call the Dispose method, or to employ the using statement in conjunction with a disposable. Sometimes a developer may not have noticed the Dispose method in the Intellisense method list. Or they may get caught up with timelines and simply miss an all-too-common bug.

The *full* implementation of the `disposable` pattern depends on providing a finalizer to call the `Dispose` method if it is not explicitly called during normal usage. Any code with unmanaged resources that does *not* have a finalizer defined could introduce memory leaks to your software. Even worse, if the developer using the object does not explicitly call `Dispose` to release the unmanaged resources *and* there is no finalizer, then the unmanaged resources may become orphaned.

```
public class Sample :IDisposable
{
 public void Dispose()
 {
    // Clean up resources
    GC.SuppressFinalize(this);
 }
 ~Sample ()
 {
    this.Dispose();
 }
}
```

**Listing 4.12:** Sample implementation of the `IDisposable` interface with the finalizer.

In this example, the `~Sample()` is the finalizer, and you may notice that the finalizer looks a lot like a destructor from C++. This often causes some confusion, but the C# finalizer is not a true destructor; it is a language implementation for the `Finalize` method. This can be an area of confusion for developers coming from a C++ background, but you can see the difference if you look at how the above code gets translated by Reflector with no optimizations defined.

```
public class Sample1 : IDisposable
{

 public void Dispose()
 {
    GC.SuppressFinalize(this);
    return;
 }
```

```
protected override void Finalize()
{
Label_0000:
  try
  {
   this.Dispose();
   goto Label_0013;
  }
  finally
  {
  Label_000B:
   base.Finalize();
  }
Label_0013:
  return;
 }
}
```

**Listing 4.13:** The underlying implementation of a finalizer.

The correct approach is to use the C++ style destructor syntax, but remember that this is *not* a C++ finalizer. A destructor is responsible for reclaiming all of the resources, whereas the finalizer only needs to worry about calling the Dispose method. The second big difference is that the finalizer is not deterministic. A true destructor is implicitly called as soon as the object goes out of scope, but a finalizer is called as a part of garbage collecting an object that has defined a finalizer. We will see, later, that *when* the finalizer is actually called is even less well defined than when the GC runs. You cannot make any assumptions about when the finalizer will run.

To make sure this all runs smoothly when finalizers are correctly implemented, the GC keeps track of the objects with finalizers. When such an object is created, a reference to it is added to the **finalization** queue, a structure maintained internal to the GC, which keeps track of the objects that need to have their finalizer called. When an object in the finalization queue is collected, the GC checks to see if it needs to call the Finalize method. If it does, the GC will explicitly call the finalizer – we'll come back to that process in just a moment. If the finalizer does not need to be called, then the object will be immediately collected.

When the GC needs to call an object's finalizer, it will be added to the `fReachable` queue, another structure maintained by the GC. At this point, the object is reachable only through the `fReachable` queue, which becomes the only root to the object. Essentially, at this point, the object has been collected (since only the GC can access it) but the finalizer has not been called and allocated resources have not been reclaimed. The finalizer will be called the next time the GC runs in a separate, high-priority thread spawned by the GC.

This has a couple of implications that we need to be aware of. To start with, the GC will have to deal with our object twice (once to make its initial collection attempt, and once to *actually* collect it – a third time if you consider the call to the finalizer), which is unnecessarily resource-intensive. The other important thing to bear in mind is that our finalizer will not be called from the same thread that the object was created in. This means that you should not make any assumptions about the running thread when the finalizer is called.

Clearly, we want to avoid having objects added to the `fReachable` queue.

To make sure that the object is *not* placed in the `fReachable` queue, the GC must be informed that finalization should be suppressed after `Dispose` is called. So, in addition to cleaning up the unmanaged resources, be sure to call `GC.SuppressFinalize(this)` to tell the GC to *not* run the finalizer.

If you remember to do that then, as long as the developer using your class calls the `Dispose` method, all of your unmanaged resources will be cleaned up and we have not added any extra load to the GC. Even if the developer *doesn't* call `Dispose`, we are still protected from orphaned resources; life is just a little harder for the GC, and we have to wait a little later for the resources to be cleared up.

# Simple Value Types

Simple value types have special representation and are directly supported by the virtual execution system. Many are frequently used, and the chart in Table 4.1 will help determine the size of each.

| Category | Bits | Type | Description |
|---|---|---|---|
| Integral types | 32* | System.Boolean | True/False |
| | 16 | System.Char | Unicode 16-bit character |
| | 8 | System.SByte | Signed 8-bit integer |
| | 16 | System.Int16 | Signed 16-bit integer |
| | 32 | System.Int32 | Signed 32-bit integer |
| | 64 | System.Int64 | Signed 64-bit integer |
| | 32/64 | System.IntPtr | Signed native integer |
| | 8 | System.Byte | Unsigned 8-bit integer |
| | 16 | System.UInt16 | Unsigned 16-bit integer |
| | 32 | System.UInt32 | Unsigned 32-bit integer |
| | 64 | System.UInt64 | Unsigned 64-bit integer |
| | 32/64 | System.UIntPtr | Unsigned native integer |
| Floating point types | 32 | System.Single | 32-bit float |
| | 64 | System.Double | 64-bit float |
| Typed reference | 64/128 | System.TypedReference | Pointer and exact type |

**Table 4.1:** Comparison of various value types.

# System.Boolean

Although `System.Boolean` is an integral type at the CLI level, C# provides no conversion to and from `int`. C++ does provide this functionality: `false` is treated as 0 and `true` is treated as 1. This is important from an interoperability perspective.

This is significant because, while `System.Boolean` is 1 byte (8 bits) in managed code, when marshaled to Windows it will be converted to the native Windows BOOL format, which is 4 bytes. Marshaling refers to converting blocks of memory from managed to unmanaged code.

```
Assert.AreEqual(1, sizeof(Boolean));
Assert.AreEqual(4, Marshal.SizeOf(new Boolean()));
```

**Listing 4.14:** Some surprises on the size of a Boolean.

The size of a Boolean may seem a little surprising. Since it has two possible values, you would expect it to be a single bit. The extra size has more to do with performance than with memory efficiency, as the extra space is used to resolve alignment issues and speed up data access. If you have a struct or object with lots of `Boolean` fields, you may want to consider a `BitVector32`, but this will introduce more complex code. You need to make sure that the memory gains justify this extra complexity.

# System.Char

`System.Char` is 2 bytes but `Marshal.SizeOf` reports it as 1 byte. `System.Char` is Unicode, whereas a Windows char is your standard ASCII character. This is important if you are supporting non-English characters. This size difference can create interoperability problems and may throw off your estimates for how much memory will be used if you expect each character to be a single byte.

```
Assert.AreEqual(2, sizeof(Char));
Assert.AreEqual(1, Marshal.SizeOf(new Char()));
```

**Listing 4.15:** Comparing the sizes of chars in managed and unmanaged code.

# Overflow checking

The .NET framework can do automatic arithmetic overflow checking to ensure that calculations are not corrupted by overflowing the values in the underlying type system. By default this is disabled in C#. Ironically, this is enabled by default for a VB.NET project, but there is little risk from disabling it in most cases. As you will see below, the right set of conditions have to be met to even have a risk of an overflow.

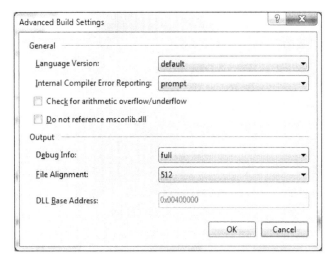

**Figure 4.2:** You can explicitly enable/disable overflow checking.

The maximum value of `System.Int32` is 2,147,483,647. What is the value when you add `Int32.MaxValue` to itself? Well, the compiler is smart enough to throw a compile-time error: *The operation overflows at compile time in checked mode.* Of course, the compiler can easily be confused. Let's add a method (see Listing 4.16).

```
public int ForceAnError()
{
 return Int32.MaxValue + Int32.MaxValue;
}
public int Add(int x, int y)
{
 return x + y;
}
```

**Listing 4.16:** Forcing an overflow exception.

The `ForceAnError` method will generate a compile-time error even though the **Check for overflow/underflow** option is not checked. This is a runtime setting and this error can be detected at compile time. This advanced build setting is intended only to avoid the overhead of an unnecessary check.

Now we call the `add` method, passing in `Int32.MaxValue` for both parameters. We don't get a compile-time error because the compiler is simply not that smart, but we also don't get the expected result. We get an overflow calculation and the wrong answer. What answer do we get? Amazingly, we get -2.

Overflowing `Int32.MaxValue` by 1 will make the variable `Int32.MinValue`, -2,147,483,648. That leaves 2,147,483,646 left in the second variable. Add them together to get -2. The reason why `Int32.MaxValue` + 1 results in `Int32.MinValue` is because of "Two's Complement" arithmetic. This is how negative numbers are represented in a binary system. In a Two's Complement representation, the Most Significant Bit (MSB) in the number is always 1. A positive number has the normal binary representation for the number with leading zeros to fill up to the MSB. To convert this to a negative number, the bits are inverted with a bitwise **NOT** operation. We then add 1 to the resulting value. In binary, `Int32.MaxValue` = 0111 1111 1111 1111 1111 1111 1111 1111. Following this formula, `Int32.MinValue` = 1000 0000 0000 0000 0000 0000 0000 0000. Looking at the two values in binary, you can hopefully see how adding 1 to `Int32.MaxValue` results in `Int32.MinValue`.

```
Assert.AreEqual(-2, Add(Int32.MaxValue, Int32.MaxValue));
```

**Listing 4.17:** The surprising result of adding Max Int to itself.

Such overflows are allowed for performance reasons, but they can lead to logical bugs that would be difficult to track down. You have the option to enable the check for overflow/ underflow at the assembly level, and then every calculation that takes place in that assembly will be checked. Alternatively, when performance is preferred but some operations should be checked, use the checked keyword to check specific calculations without incurring this extra cost everywhere.

```
public int Add(int x, int y)
{
  return checked(x + y);
}
```

**Listing 4.18:** Explicitly checking a key calculation for overflow.

An OverflowException is now thrown at runtime when the above method is called passing in MaxValue for the parameters. If you really want to allow for overflowing, such as adding Int32.MaxValue to itself, there's a corresponding unchecked keyword.

# Strings

Strings are reference types that behave in many ways like a value type. Assignment and comparison works as you would expect with a value type, because they have value equality implemented, and sometimes they may even have the same reference but, in general, they will behave more like value types. This is a likely source of bugs among novice programmers, since the behavior may not be immediately obvious.

```
public void Test()
{
 string s = "Original";
 s.ToLower();
 if (object.ReferenceEquals(s, "Original"))
   Console.WriteLine("They have the same reference");
 else
   Console.WriteLine("They do not have the same reference");
 s = s.ToLower();
 if (object.ReferenceEquals( s, "original"))
   Console.WriteLine("They have the same reference");
 else
   Console.WriteLine("They do not have the same reference");
}
```

**Listing 4.19:** Showing the effects of immutable strings on reference equality.

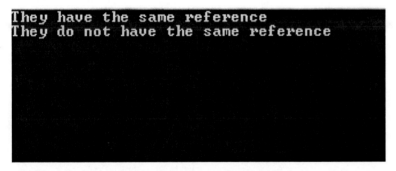

**Figure 4.3:** The output from the code in Listing 4.19.

The output is unexpected. The confusion here lies in understanding mutability, rather than reference versus value types. Since strings are immutable, methods from the `string` class return a new string rather than modify the original string's memory. This can both improve code quality by reducing side effects, and reduce performance if you are not careful.

The first pair of strings has the same reference, because of interning, which we will explain later. The second pair of strings does not have the same reference, because the `ToLower` method created a new object.

109

The value for a string is stored in the heap. This is important because the stack can only hold 1 MB, and it would not be very difficult to imagine a single string using all of that space.

This string immutability can potentially create other memory usage issues. Every method call will result in a new string, and the old string will need to be garbage collected. In most cases, there will be no references to the old string, but the memory will not be reclaimed until the GC runs. Even though this memory will be reclaimed, the result is that the GC will need to run more frequently.

# Intern pool

When comparing the identity of a string literal, you may be surprised to discover that they can have the same reference, despite having two unique declarations. We saw this earlier, in Listing 4.4.

```
string first = "text";
string second = "text";
bool areSame = object.ReferenceEquals(first, second);
Assert.IsTrue(areSame);
```

**Listing 4.20** Two strings can have the same reference even when they are declared separately.

Strings are reference types, so it is not apparent that this would be true. In fact, if these strings were never written as string literals in the program, `Object.ReferenceEquals` would be false. Since the strings were written as string literals, they are stored in the **intern pool** by the CLR.

The intern pool is an optimization to speed up string literal comparisons. Using Reflector, we see that `String.Equals` has the implementation shown in Listing 4.21. The `EqualsHelper` is a private method in the String class using unsafe pointer manipulation to optimize the string comparison.

```
public static bool Equals(string a, string b)
{
 return ((a == b) ||
    (((a != null) && (b != null)) && EqualsHelper(a, b)));
}
```

**Listing 4.21:** Implementation of the `Equals` method in the String class.

In the case of matching interned strings, the comparison stops at a==b, which can potentially be a substantial performance boost (especially when comparing large strings). The implementation of `EqualsHelper` first checks to see if the references are the same. If they are, the comparison can conclude with success.

You can retrieve an instance from the intern pool with the `String.IsInterned` method, which will return null if the string is not in the pool. The `String.Intern` method will check the pool, add the string if it's not there, and return a reference to the string from the pool.

```
string first = String.Intern(String.Concat("auto", "dog"));
string second = String.IsInterned(String.Concat("auto", "dog"));

Assert.AreSame(first, second);
```

**Listing 4.22:** Showing the effects of explicitly interning a string.

While string literals are automatically added to the intern pool, instances of strings are not. They must be explicitly added with a call to `String.Intern`.

This sounds like a great way to improve the performance of your application, but be careful. There are important memory considerations. Items in the intern pool are not likely to be garbage collected. These references are accessible throughout the CLR and so can survive your application, and can survive every scope within your application. Another important factor is that the string is created separate from the intern pool before it is added to the pool. This will increase the overall memory footprint.

So, adding many strings to the intern pool could substantially increase your memory footprint and this segment of memory will not be reclaimed until you recycle the entire run time.

If you feel that string interning is adversely affecting the memory management in your application, you can disable it in individual assemblies with the `CompilationRelaxationsAttribute`.

# Concatenation

A common task when working with strings is adding them together. The `string` class has an operator overload for + that converts the call to a `String.Concat`. The C# compiler optimizes the code by concatenating string literals. So Listing 4.23 is optimized as shown in Listing 4.24.

```
string panda = "bear" + "cat";
```

**Listing 4.23:** A common string concatenation.

```
string panda = "bearcat";
```

**Listing 4.24:** How the compiler will optimize it.

The compiler also converts concatenation with variables and non-string literals into a call to `String.Concat`. So Listing 4.25 becomes Listing 4.26.

```
string panda = "bear";
panda += "cat";
```

**Listing 4.25:** Forcing the compiler to concatenate.

```
string panda = "bear";
panda = String.Concat(panda, "cat");
```

**Listing 4.26:** The compiler explicitly calling the `String.Concat` method.

As you can see, the compiler is doing its best to help out the developer, but this is not without pitfalls. For example, perhaps the most pervasive challenge with string concatenation involves building a large string composed of many known elements. Approaching this problem with simple concatenation techniques leads to the creation of many small objects that must be garbage collected, potentially incurring unnecessary cost (see Listing 4.27).

```
public static string SerializeGeometry(IEnumerable<GeographicPoint> points)
{
  string result = "<Coordinates>";

 foreach (var point in points)
 {
   result += "\t<Coordinate>" + point + "</Coordinate>";
 }

 result += "<Coordinate>";
 return result;
}
```

**Listing 4.27:** String concatenation in a loop.

The `SerializeGeometry` method creates an XML string based on an `IEnumerable` of `GeographicPoint`. There are an unknown number of elements in the sequence, as it is iterated, appending as many strings as needed to the resulting variable. Since `string` is immutable, this causes a new string to be allocated at every pass through the loop. This problem can be prevented by using the `StringBuilder` class.

```
public static string SerializeGeometry(IEnumerable<GeographicPoint> points)
{
  StringBuilder result = new StringBuilder();
  result.AppendLine("<Coordinates>");

  foreach (var point in points)
  {
    result.AppendLine("\t<Coordinate>" + point + "</Coordinate>");
  }

  result.AppendLine("<Coordinate>");
  return result.ToString();
}
```

**Listing 4.28:** Using `StringBuilder` in a loop.

`StringBuilder` will build the string with a single object for the GC to have to keep track of. This will not only reduce the total memory footprint, but also simplify the job that the GC has to do.

Naturally, we also need to be careful when using the `StringBuilder`, as there is a fair amount of logic in it. Thus, in simple cases, it can be overkill and adversely impact performance. As a good rule of thumb, you should probably never use a `StringBuilder` outside of a loop. Also don't do any string concatenation inside of the calls to the Append method, as this will just reintroduce the problems with multiple objects that we are trying to avoid in the first place.

# Structs

The struct type is a fundamental, user-defined value type. In C#, this type is defined with the `struct` keyword. It should be used sparingly, and only when the type represents a single value consisting of 16 bytes or more. It should also be immutable, and like all value types, infrequently boxed.

You may wonder about the 16 byte limit, especially since this restriction is not enforced. The reasoning comes from the overhead of creating an object. On a 32-bit machine, 12 bytes are used just for overhead – an 8-byte header and a 4-byte reference. Therefore, when an object does not have at least 16 bytes of data, you may have a very inefficient design. Consider converting such objects to structs which do not have such heavy overhead.

Even though structs can be larger than 16 bytes, we want to be careful with how large they get to be. Structs are created on the stack rather than the heap. Performance is enhanced when moving smaller data structures around on the stack. If the struct represents an atomic value, this is usually not an issue. However, those wishing to gain value semantics on a large object quickly run into memory issues.

Structs inherit from `System.Struct` and cannot be further inherited. This may limit your design options since structs cannot have a custom-defined base class and cannot have any derived classes. A default constructor is provided by the CLR and cannot be custom defined, and field values cannot be initialized. This requires the struct to be valid with an initial state for all of its members.

Even though a struct cannot participate in inheritance, it can implement an interface. You need to be careful doing this, though; type casting a struct to an interface implicitly boxes the struct, which incurs the overhead of boxing and unboxing, and also has an interesting side effect.

If you type cast a struct to an interface and then perform operations on the interface, the original struct is not affected. This can lead to very subtle logic errors and cause much confusion. The problem is that the interface now refers to a "boxed" copy of the original struct, and not to the same bits that the original struct occupied. Consider the example in Listing 4.29, where we define a simple interface and a struct as well as a class that implements the interface.

```
public interface IShape
{
 Point Top { get; set; }
 void Move(Point newLocation);
}

public struct SimpleShape : IShape
{
 public Point Top
 {
   get; set;
 }

 public void Move(Point newLocation)
 {
   Top = newLocation;
 }
}

public class ClassShape : IShape
{
 public Point Top
 {
   get; set;
 }

 public void Move(Point newLocation)
 {
   Top = newLocation;
 }
}
```

**Listing 4.29:** A struct and a class implementing a common interface.

Notice that the interface and the class have the exact same implementation. In the example in Listing 4.30, notice how different the output is.

```
var shape = new SimpleShape();
shape.Top = new Point(10, 20);
var classShape = new ClassShape();
classShape.Top = new Point(40, 50);
IShape iShape = shape as IShape;
iShape.Move(new Point(4, 4));
IShape iClassShape = classShape as IShape;
iClassShape.Move(new Point( 110, 110));
Console.WriteLine("Shape: " +shape.Top);
Console.WriteLine("iShape: " +iShape.Top);
Console.WriteLine("classShape: " + classShape.Top);
Console.WriteLine("iClassShape: " + iClassShape.Top);
```

**Listing 4.30:** Structs are value types and boxing creates a new copy in the reference.

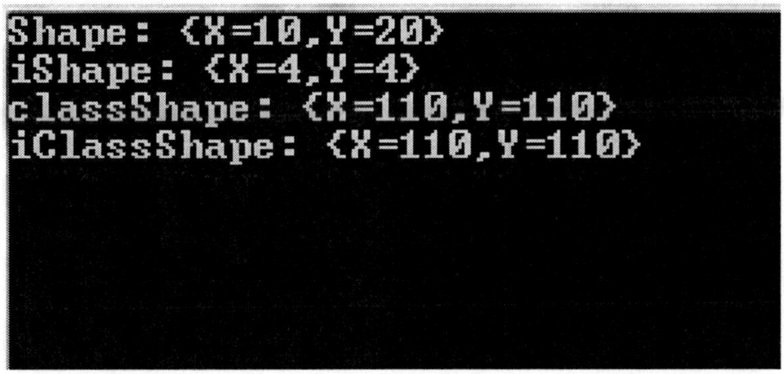

```
Shape: {X=10,Y=20}
iShape: {X=4,Y=4}
classShape: {X=110,Y=110}
iClassShape: {X=110,Y=110}
```

**Figure 4.4:**   You would expect Shape and iShape to have the same values, but they won't.

Because of boxing, Shape and iShape refer to different memory locations. They now have different values because the processing is done on different entities. On the other hand, with the class, classShape and iClassShape refer to the same entity, and updates to one affect both. This is the expected behavior for both cases. The unexpected behavior with the struct can lead to subtle logic errors.

This illustrates the importance of immutability for structs. An immutable object is one whose values cannot be modified after creation. For an example of this, look at the example of the DateTime struct in Listing 4.31.

```
DateTime today = DateTime.Today;
DateTime tomorrow = today.AddDays(1);
```

**Listing 4.31:** Structs need to be immutable.


Although `DateTime` has a `Day` property, it is read-only. To add a day to a `DateTime`, the `AddDays()` method must be called, which returns a *new* `DateTime`, while the original `DateTime` retains its value.

This has several advantages, not least of which is that an immutable struct will not be subject to the boxing issue we just saw. A `DateTime` value is thread-safe since different threads will always receive the same value; if a `DateTime` is stored in a `HashTable` or other hash-based collection, there is no danger of its state (and therefore its value) being changed while occupying another value's location. If you have these issues, it would be wise to make your structs immutable.

Listing 4.32 is an example of a `GeographicPoint` class that is not immutable.

```
public partial struct GeographicPoint
{
  private float latitude;
  private float longitude;
  private int altitude;

  public float Latitude
  {
    get { return latitude; }
    set { latitude = value; }
  }

  public float Longitude
  {
    get { return longitude; }
    set { longitude = value; }
  }

  public int Altitude
```

```
    {
      get { return altitude; }
      set { altitude = value; }
    }


    public GeographicPoint(float latitude, float longitude, int altitude)
    {

      this.latitude = latitude;
      this.longitude = longitude;
      this.altitude = altitude;
    }
  }
```

**Listing 4.32:** `GeographicPoint` is not immutable and, as a struct, will cause problems.


This struct can be made immutable by making its fields read-only and removing the property setters. In other projects, it will be necessary to modify any method mutating the state of the instance so that it no longer does so. That will require refactoring (Listing 4.33) to use local variables or returning new instances of the struct.

```
  public partial struct GeographicPoint
  {
    private readonly float latitude;
    private readonly float longitude;
    private readonly int altitude;

    public float Latitude
    {
      get { return latitude; }
    }

    public float Longitude
    {
      get { return longitude; }
    }

    public int Altitude
```

```
      {
        get { return altitude; }
      }
      public GeographicPoint(float latitude, float longitude, int altitude)
      {
        this.latitude = latitude;
        this.longitude = longitude;
        this.altitude = altitude;
      }
      public GeographicPoint ChangeLatitude (float newLatitude)
      {
        return new GeographicPoint(latitude, Longitude, Altitude);
      }
      public GeographicPoint ChangeLongitude (float newLongitude)
      {
        return new GeographicPoint(Latitude, newLongitude, Altitude);
      }
    }
```

**Listing 4.33:** Making the GeographicPoint struct immutable.

Although this struct is now immutable, it will still have an issue with Hashtables. When struct objects are used as Hashtable keys, the lookup operation for the Hashtable is slower because of the implementation of the GetHashCode method used to perform the lookup. When a struct contains only simple value types (int, short, etc.) the default implementation of GetHashCode inherited from System.Object causes most of the keys to be stored in the same location. When multiple keys hash to the same location, the hash table must do collision resolution to find the correct entry. In extreme cases, you may have to search out every entry in the Hashtable to confirm that your item is not there. To resolve this problem, we need to override Object.GetHashCode() to ensure proper storage. We should also override Object.Equals() in the process. The default Object.Equals() works, and we could leave it alone. However, it is rather slow because it uses reflection to check each property. By implementing our own Equals() method we can optimize it and eliminate reflection and boxing. While we're implementing the overridden instance Equals(), we should complete the struct by implementing the other equality operators, == and != (see Listing 4.34).

```csharp
public partial struct GeographicPoint
{
  public static bool operator ==(GeographicPoint first, GeographicPoint second)
  {
    return first.Equals(second);
  }

  public static bool operator !=(GeographicPoint first, GeographicPoint second)
  {
    return !first.Equals(second);
  }

  public override int GetHashCode()
  {
    return (int)this.latitude ^ (int)this.longitude ^ this.altitude;
  }

  public override bool Equals(object obj)
  {
    if (obj is GeographicPoint)
    {
     return Equals((GeographicPoint)obj);
    }

    return false;
  }

  public bool Equals(GeographicPoint other)
  {
    return this.latitude == other.latitude
      && this.longitude == other.longitude
      && this.altitude == other.altitude;
  }
}
```

**Listing 4.34:** A fully implemented GeographicPoint optimized for hashing and safe from boxing errors.

With the struct fully implemented, we now have more useful semantics. We can now ensure GeographicPoint is thread-safe, Hashtable friendly, and works with equality operators.

# Classes

When people think of object-oriented programming, they typically imagine defining and instantiating classes. Of course, the `Class` type is but one of many types in the .NET framework, but it is the most common user-constructed type.

Classes are reference types, and it is a common mistake to create a class when value semantics are desired. If the class represents an immutable atomic value, consider a struct instead. Of course, there are also allocation considerations when creating any object. Reference types must have memory allocated when an instance is created, whereas value types (such as structs) are allocated memory as soon as they are created.

# Size of an Object

Object sizes are determined by their field values, as laid out in the *Simple Value Types* section earlier, but are often padded for performance reasons. Value types are in-lined with the object, and reference types have a `TypedReference` value allocated which will likely point to the heap. Both reference types and value types provide control over their layout in memory and the size of the padding between fields.

We may need to control the layout of an object when interacting with unmanaged code. Since reference types are not very compatible with unmanaged code, you will normally need to achieve this with structs. There may be cases where you wish to change a class structure as well, and this information applies to both.

The `System.Runtime.InteropServices.StructLayoutAttribute` class controls how fields are laid out in memory. Despite its name, this attribute can be used to influence the structure of both classes and structs. Its constructor takes the `LayoutKind` enum. By default in C# and VB.NET, structs are marked as `LayoutKind.Sequential`, meaning that fields are defined in memory in the order defined in code.

The `Size` field dictates the absolute size of the object; memory beyond the defined fields is typically accessed with unmanaged code. The `CharSet` field determines the string marshaling: whether strings will be converted to `LPWSTR` or `LPSTR` (Long Pointer to Wide String or Long Pointer to String). `LPWSTR` should be used for UNICODE strings. `LPSTR` is used for a regular array of 8-bit characters. By default, strings in the Framework are stored as UTF-16, and those in Windows are Unicode or ANSI. Setting `CharSet.Auto` chooses the appropriate encoding based upon the platform. This will often be needed to facilitate COM interop.

The `Pack` field sets the memory boundaries for `LayoutKind.Sequential`. Setting `Pack` with a value of 0 will choose the default for the platform, while setting it to 1 will ensure there are no boundaries between each field in memory. Pack settings 2, 4, 8, 16, 32, 64, and 128 lay out the fields on memory offsets relative to the address of the first field. `Pack` sizes larger than that processor's boundary are substituted for the processor boundary size, which provides a performance penalty for the processor. For reference, an Intel processor's boundary sizes are 4 bytes. This may be relevant when exporting a structure (sending over the network, writing to disk, using p/invoke and `interop`, etc.), to ensure that the layout is consistent.

You might think you could use this internally to reduce memory usage (by reducing the pack size). In fact, it might do that, but there could also be a significant performance hit on some hardware, while on other hardware it might not even work, due to unaligned access to the data (though I don't believe this applies to anything .NET runs on). This is *not* a recommended strategy for reducing memory usage, and should only be used to solve a specific problem with exporting an object.

Consider the code in Listing 4.35. Even though the objects of this type may take up less memory than they would without the `StructLayout` attribute, code accessing this struct will suffer a performance penalty. How much of a performance penalty depends on your hardware and the underlying data types.

```
[StructLayout(LayoutKind.Sequential, Pack = 0)]
public struct Sequential
{
  private byte b;
  private char c;
  private float f;
  private int i;

  public byte Byte
  {
    get { return b; }
    set { b = value; }
  }

  public char Char
  {
    get { return c; }
    set { c = value; }
  }

  public float Float
  {
    get { return f; }
    set { f = value; }
  }

  public int Integer
  {
    get { return i; }
    set { i = value; }
  }

}
```

**Listing 4.35:** Struct layout with no packing. May slow down memory retrieval.


The LayoutKind.Explicit value gives you full control over your data. However, you should have a good reason for doing this, such as calling unmanaged code that explicitly needs data laid out in a specific manner, as this process is error prone and could lead to data corruption. Listing 4.36 gives an example.

```
[StructLayout(LayoutKind.Explicit)]
public struct Union
{
  [FieldOffset(0)]
  private byte b;

  [FieldOffset(0)]
  private char c;

  [FieldOffset(0)]
  private float f;

  [FieldOffset(0)]
  private int i;

  public byte Byte
  {
    get { return b; }
    set { b = value; }
  }

  public char Char
  {
    get { return c; }
    set { c = value; }
  }

  public float Float
  {
    get { return f; }
    set { f = value; }
  }

  public int Integer
  {
    get { return i; }
    set { i = value; }
  }
}
```

**Listing 4.36:** A struct explicitly setting all fields to point to the same memory location.

With the `Union` struct, you can modify the value in one field and affect the value of another field. This is because the `FieldOffset` attributes point all of the fields to the same location.

```
static void Main(string[] args)
  {
  var union = new Union();
  union.Char = 'W';
  Console.WriteLine("Union.Byte: " + union.Byte);
  Console.WriteLine("Union.Char: " + union.Char);
  Console.WriteLine("Union.Float: " + union.Float);
  Console.WriteLine("Union.Integer: " + union.Integer);
  }
```

**Listing 4.37:** We explicitly set the value of `Char` but all fields now have a value.

```
Union.Byte: 87
Union.Char: W
Union.Float: 1.21913E-43
Union.Integer: 87
```

**Figure 4.5:**   The bits at this memory location are interpreted according to the rules for the various types.

We assigned a valid value for one of the fields, and the other fields interpret the bits in the shared location as a valid value in their respective datatypes. W has an ASCII value of 87, which has a valid value as a byte and an integer. On the other hand, the interpreted value for the `Float` is truly bizarre.

If that wasn't wild enough, you can use this to point reference types at the same memory space in managed code. This is not something I recommend, but just be aware that it can be done (this is almost guaranteed to create a logic error and at the very least result in some very confusing code).

```
public class Person
{
 public string FirstName { get; set; }
 public string LastName { get; set; }
}

public class Place
{
 public string City { get; set; }
 public string Country { get; set; }
}

[StructLayout(LayoutKind.Explicit)]
public struct NoCasting
{
 [FieldOffset(0)]
 private Person person;

 [FieldOffset(0)]
 private Place place;

 public Person Person
 {
   get { return person; }
   set { person = value; }
 }

 public Place Place
 {
   get { return place; }
   set { place = value; }
 }
}
```

**Listing 4.38:** The Person and Place properties will refer to the same set of bits.

In the example in Listing 4.38, both **Person** and **Place** will refer back to the same set of bits allocated to the **NoCasting** object.

```
NoCasting noCasting = new NoCasting
{
 Person = new Person { FirstName = "Fada", LastName = "Chad" }
};
Console.WriteLine("noCasting.Person:\t"
        + noCasting.Person.FirstName + " " + noCasting.Person.LastName);
Console.WriteLine("noCasting.Place:\t"
        + noCasting.Place.City + " in " + noCasting.Place.Country);
```

**Listing 4.39:** Updating one property will result in both properties being updated.

**Figure 4.6:**   This is almost guaranteed not to be the expected result.

You can assign the **Person** or **Place** property on a **NoCasting** instance at any time, and it will point the other property at the same member space. They don't inherit from each other, and you can't cast one to the other. The only reason this makes any sense is because the field layout is the same. If you were to rely on programming paradigms such as this, it would only take a field reordering to break your code.

This is fascinating and definitely produces some bizarre behavior. It also has no place in code that you plan to run in production. It is fun for a demonstration or to confuse the unsuspecting, but it will eventually create a logic error that will be difficult to track down.

Unless you have very specific marshaling requirements and you know exactly what you are doing, leave the **StructureLayout** alone. This is not a good way to squeeze out better memory management, and will almost always lead to performance problems or logic errors.

# Delegates

Executable code typically exists as a method belonging to a static, or instance of a struct or class. A delegate is another reference type that represents a method, similar to a function pointer in other languages. However, delegates are type-safe and secure, providing object-oriented functions.

Delegates in C# and VB.NET inherit from `System.MulticastDelegate` (which inherits from `System.Delegate` and, in turn, from `System.Object`). This class provides a linked list of delegates which are invoked synchronously in order (Listing 4.40).

```
public delegate void Function();

public void WriteInformation()
{
  Debug.WriteLine("Got Here");
}

public void CallFunction()
{
  Function function = new Function(WriteInformation);
  function();
}
```

**Listing 4.40:** Declare a delegate and associate a method with it.

Parameters can be added to a delegate, which are then necessary for the invocation of the method the delegate is instantiated with, as well as the delegate itself (Listing 4.41).

```
public delegate void Function(string info);

public void WriteInformation(string info)
{
  Debug.WriteLine(info);
}
```

```
public void CallFunction()
{
 Function function = new Function(WriteInformation);
 function("function called");
}
```

**Listing 4.41:** Declare a delegate with parameters and associate a method with it.

Delegates can be combined by calling the `Delegate.Combine` method, although the semantics of the delegate are then lost and it must be invoked through the `Dynamic-Invoke()` method, as shown in Listing 4.42.

```
public delegate void Function(string info);

public void WriteInformation(string info)
{
 Debug.WriteLine(info);
}

public void WriteToConsole(string info)
{
 Console.WriteLine(info);
}

public void CallFunction()
{
 Function function = new Function(WriteInformation);
 Function another = new Function(WriteToConsole);
 var del = Delegate.Combine(function, another);
 del.DynamicInvoke("multicast");
}
```

**Listing 4.42:** Associating multiple methods with a delegate.

Be aware that when a multicast delegate is invoked, the delegates in the invocation list are called synchronously in the order in which they appear. If an error occurs during execution of the list, an exception is thrown.

This ability is useful for writing reusable delegates, but oftentimes delegates are scoped within a method. The concept of anonymous methods shown in Listing 4.43 was introduced as an alternative to named methods.

```
public delegate void Function(string info);

public void CallFunction()
{
  Function function = delegate(string info) { Debug.WriteLine(info); };
  function("This method is anonymous");
}
```

Listing 4.43: Associating an anonymous method with a delegate.

More innovations in the .NET languages took place, and anonymous functions were introduced. Lambda expressions further reduced the amount of typing necessary to create a delegate. In addition, standardized, generic delegate types were introduced to the .NET framework to easily create delegates when necessary. Delegates without return types are known as Actions, and those with return types are known as Funcs. The last generic parameter of a Func type is the return type.

```
Action<string> function = info => Debug.WriteLine(info);
function("Created from a lambda");
```

Listing 4.44: A simple lambda action.

Despite the progression of delegate usage in the .NET languages, the story behind the scenes remains largely the same. The compiler creates a static delegate definition and a named method, and places the code contained within the lambda expression inside of that named method. It then creates the delegate, if it does not already exist, and calls it. Anonymous methods and functions are really just syntactic sugar.

A common use of delegates is for event handlers, as they allow you to loosely couple functionality through an event model. The classic example of this is performing an action when a button is clicked, shown in Listing 4.45 and Figure 4.7.

```
public MainWindow()
{
  InitializeComponent();
  button.Click += (sender, e) => MessageBox.Show("Under the Hood");
}
```

**Listing 4.45:** Wiring up an event handler to an anonymous method.

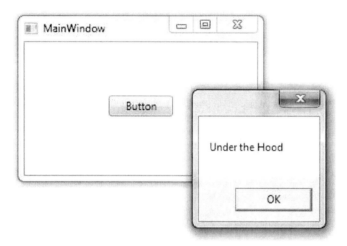

**Figure 4.7:**   The outcome from Listing 4.45.

Notice the operator that adds the lambda expression to the `Click` event. Event handlers are added to an event list, ready to be invoked, and it is important to release the delegates in the event list, or set the event to null when disposing of the object (and classes that implement events should implement `IDisposable`). This might seem like stating the obvious, and the situation isn't so bad when only one object has a reference to the delegate. However, if more than one object has a reference to the same delegate, they will all be kept alive until all the objects with a reference to the same delegate are released. We will explore this more fully in Chapter 5.

# Closures

Variables that are created outside of an anonymous method but used within it are captured in a closure. This allows the delegate to have access to the value even when the variable goes out of scope.

```
string str = "Original";
Action writeLine = () => Console.WriteLine(str);
writeLine();

str = "Changed";
writeLine();
```

**Listing 4.46:** A very simple closure.

From reading the code in Listing 4.46 it is expected that it will first write "Original" to the screen, followed by "Changed". That is exactly how it works, which perhaps seems odd in light of the fact that string is immutable and it has already been passed into the delegate.

What happens is that the compiler does the heavy lifting for you, creating a class and assigning the values to it. This will actually affect you any time you use an outside variable inside of an anonymous method or function. Consider the slightly more complex closure in Listing 4.47.

```
public Person WhoReportsTo (List<Employee > data, Person targetEmployee)
{
  return data.Find(d => d.ReportsTo == targetEmployee);
}
```

**Listing 4.47:** A more complex example with closures.

Once the compiler works its magic, we get the code in Listing 4.48.

```
[CompilerGenerated]
private sealed class <>c__DisplayClass4
{
 // Fields
 public Person targetEmployee;

 // Methods
 public bool <WhoReportsTo>b__3(Employee d)
 {
   return (d.ReportsTo == this.targetEmployee);
 }
}
```

**Listing 4.48:** The dynamic class generated enclosing the captured variables.

The anonymous method is actually "enclosed" in a dynamic compiler-generated class, which includes a member variable for every external variable that the anonymous method references. This generated class and all enclosed variables will stay alive as long as the delegate is accessible. This extended lifetime can dramatically delay when variables are eligible for garbage collection, and thus create situations that look like a memory leak.

Avoid closures with memory intensive variables.

# Effects of Yield

In C#, the `yield` keyword is used to generate an implementation of the `Iterator` pattern, which in .NET is an implementation of `IEnumerator`. It is a useful and under-utilized feature of the C# language that can greatly reduce the complexity of iterating lazy or dynamic collections of objects. Methods using the `yield` keyword must return `IEnumerable`, `IEnumerable<T>`, `IEnumerator`, or `IEnumerator<T>`. For type-safety and semantics, it is often preferred to return `IEnumerable<T>`.

What actually happens behind the scenes with a `yield` statement is often hard to understand. The compiler will take your method that uses a `yield` statement and translate it into a class that implements the logic in your method. This class implements the `Iterator` pattern, and each time the iterator is called (the `MoveNext` method), your original method is called again. When the `yield` statement is hit, the `MoveNext` method returns. This means that your method will be called once for each element that will ultimately be returned. The generated code keeps track of state between calls to your method.

This has a couple of advantages. The most important, from a memory perspective, is that you never have to declare the list that the calling code will appear to loop through. Only one item at a time has to be in memory, which can be a dramatic improvement if only one object is used at a time. With the `yield` statement, you can write the logic in a more natural way, as if all of the processing was done in a single method call, and let the compiler handle the state processing across multiple method calls.

Consider the example in Listing 4.49. The processing logic is written in a natural style with a straightforward loop, but we avoid having to ever have all 360 elements in the list in memory at one time. Depending on the size of the elements in the list and the number of elements, this can be a substantial reduction in the memory footprint. Best of all, we don't have to sacrifice readability to get the performance benefits.

```
public IEnumerable <AmortizationScheduleItem> CalculatePayments
    (decimal principal, int term, decimal interestRate,
     decimal monthlyPayment, DateTime startingDate)
{
 decimal totalInterest = 0;
 decimal balanceamount = principal;
 for (int count = 0; count <= term - 1; count++)
 {
   decimal monthInterest = principal*
     ((interestRate/100m)*(1.0m/12.0m));
   decimal monthPrincipal = monthlyPayment - monthInterest;
   totalInterest += monthInterest;
   principal -= monthPrincipal;
   balanceamount = balanceamount - monthPrincipal;
```

Chapter 4: Common Memory Problems

```
    var monthlyDetail = new AmortizationScheduleItem
        {
            Date = startingDate.AddMonths(count),
            Balance = balanceamount,
            PrincipalPaid = monthPrincipal,
            InterestPaid = monthInterest,
            Payment = monthlyPayment,
            TotalInterest = totalInterest
        };
    yield return monthlyDetail;
  }
}
```

**Listing 4.49:** An intuitive payment calculator using `yield` to lower the memory footprint.

The `CalculatePayments` method uses the `yield` statement to return a result as each item is calculated. By calculating all values in a loop, we can easily keep track of intermediate values and use them to build the next result, but behind the scenes we are not running all of these calculations in a single loop. Fortunately, we can generally ignore such pesky details. The compiler takes this simple method and converts it to a class similar to Listing 4.50.

```
[CompilerGenerated]
private sealed class <CalculatePayments>d__5 : IEnumerable<AmortizationScheduleIt
em>, IEnumerable, IEnumerator<AmortizationScheduleItem>, IEnumerator, IDisposable
{
 // Fields
 private int <>1__state;
 private AmortizationScheduleItem <>2__current;
 public decimal <>3__interestRate;
 public decimal <>3__monthlyPayment;
 public decimal <>3__principal;
 public DateTime <>3__startingDate;
 public int <>3__term;
 public Program <>4__this;
 public AmortizationScheduleItem <>g__initLocal4;
 private int <>1__initialThreadId;
 public decimal <balanceamount>5__7;
 public int <count>5__8;
 public decimal <monthInterest>5__9;
```

```
public AmortizationScheduleItem <monthlyDetail>5__b;
public decimal <monthPrincipal>5__a;
public decimal <totalInterest>5__6;
public decimal interestRate;
public decimal monthlyPayment;
public decimal principal;
public DateTime startingDate;
public int term;

// Methods
[DebuggerHidden]
public <CalculatePayments>d__5(int <>1__state)
{
  this.<>1__state = <>1__state;
  this.<>1__initialThreadId = Thread.CurrentThread.ManagedThreadId;
}

private bool MoveNext()
{
  switch (this.<>1__state)
  {
  case 0:
    this.<>1__state = -1;
    this.<totalInterest>5__6 = 0M;
    this.<balanceamount>5__7 = this.principal;
    this.<count>5__8 = 0;
    while (this.<count>5__8 <= (this.term - 1))
    {
      this.<monthInterest>5__9 = this.principal *
      ((this.interestRate / 100M) * 0.08333M);
      this.<monthPrincipal>5__a = this.monthlyPayment —
       this.<monthInterest>5__9;
      this.<totalInterest>5__6 += this.<monthInterest>5__9;
      this.principal -= this.<monthPrincipal>5__a;
      this.<balanceamount>5__7 -= this.<monthPrincipal>5__a;
      this.<>g__initLocal4 = new AmortizationScheduleItem();
      this.<>g__initLocal4.Date =
       this.startingDate.AddMonths(this.<count>5__8);
      this.<>g__initLocal4.Balance =
       this.<balanceamount>5__7;
      this.<>g__initLocal4.PrincipalPaid =
       this.<monthPrincipal>5__a;
      this.<>g__initLocal4.InterestPaid =
       this.<monthInterest>5__9;
```

```
        this.<>g__initLocal4.Payment = this.monthlyPayment;
        this.<>g__initLocal4.TotalInterest =
         this.<totalInterest>5__6;
        this.<monthlyDetail>5__b = this.<>g__initLocal4;
        this.<>2__current = this.<monthlyDetail>5__b;
        this.<>1__state = 1;
        return true;
      Label_0190:
        this.<>1__state = -1;
        this.<count>5__8++;
      }
      break;

    case 1:
      goto Label_0190;
    }
    return false;
  }


[DebuggerHidden]
IEnumerator<AmortizationScheduleItem>
    IEnumerable<AmortizationScheduleItem>.GetEnumerator()
{
  Program.<CalculatePayments>d__5 d__;
  if ((Thread.CurrentThread.ManagedThreadId ==
   this.<>1__initialThreadId) && (this.<>1__state == -2))
  {
   this.<>1__state = 0;
   d__ = this;
  }
  else
  {
   d__ = new Program.<CalculatePayments>d__5(0);
   d__.<>4__this = this.<>4__this;
  }
  d__.principal = this.<>3__principal;
  d__.term = this.<>3__term;
  d__.interestRate = this.<>3__interestRate;
  d__.monthlyPayment = this.<>3__monthlyPayment;
  d__.startingDate = this.<>3__startingDate;
  return d__;
}
```

```
[DebuggerHidden]
IEnumerator IEnumerable.GetEnumerator()
{
  return this.System.Collections.Generic.
    IEnumerable<ConsoleApplication1.AmortizationScheduleItem>.
     GetEnumerator();
}

[DebuggerHidden]
void IEnumerator.Reset()
{
  throw new NotSupportedException();
}

void IDisposable.Dispose()
{
}

// Properties
AmortizationScheduleItem IEnumerator<AmortizationScheduleItem>.Current
{
  [DebuggerHidden]
  get
  {
   return this.<>2__current;
  }
}

object IEnumerator.Current
{
  [DebuggerHidden]
  get
  {
   return this.<>2__current;
  }
 }
}
```

**Listing 4.50:** The effects of the yield expanded by the compiler.

You might be forgiven for thinking "*Wow! The code generated by the compiler is complex and not at all easy to follow*," and that's exactly true. Fortunately, we don't have to write this code or worry about maintaining it. We can write the much easier-to-follow code using the `yield` statement and reap the benefits of the more complicated code that the compiler generates.

Using the code is very intuitive as well. We can treat the method as if it returns the full array and not worry about the magic happening behind the scenes.

```
foreach (var item in a.CalculatePayments(principle ,term,
  interstRate , monthlyPayment , DateTime.Today ))
{
 Console.WriteLine( string.Format( "Month: {0:d}\tBalance: " +
   "{1:c}\tInterest Paid: {2:c}\tPrincipal Paid: " +
   "{3:c}\tTotal Interest Paid: {4:c}",
   item.Date, item.Balance, item.InterestPaid ,
   item.PrincipalPaid, item.TotalInterest ));
}
```

**Listing 4.51:** Using `CalculatePayments` as if it was a "regular " iterator.

The largest impact the use of the `Iterator` pattern will have on memory and performance is making the decision on whether it is more valuable to lazily retrieve values or retain those values in memory. Lazy retrieval ensures the data is current, keeps the heap clear, but could potentially impact garbage collection with the creation of many small objects. Maintaining the data in memory is better if that data is unlikely to change, or is used more often, but it could move the larger object to a higher generation.

My recommendation is to convert iterators to collection types at application, framework, and layer boundaries. And always test with a profiler to ensure that you get the expected performance results.

# Arrays and Collections

Arrays and other collection types are reference types that contain other objects. With arrays, every item must be the same data type but, unlike the simple arrays from C or C++, arrays in .NET benefit from inheritance. All arrays derive from `System.Array`, which gives them some useful features such as the `IClonable`, `IEnumerable`, `ICollection`, and `IList` interfaces. Possibly the most exciting feature that .NET brings to the table is array index validation, which ensures that we don't access memory that has not been allocated to the array.

Such buffer overflows are a common source for security issues and exploits, but with .NET, instead of a security vulnerability to exploit, you get an `IndexOutOfRange-Exception`. Behind the scenes, the framework is checking to confirm that the index is valid with every call. Some may worry about the performance overhead of these index validation tests, although they needn't. While it *is* possible to skip this validation by compiling with the "unsafe" option, this is rarely a good option, and the overhead of doing the index validations is minimal compared to the risks of having buffer overflows.

Before generics were introduced in .NET 2.0, `ArrayLists` were the most widely used collection type object, and they have a couple of differences from the humble array. Most notably, the `ArrayList` does not require that all elements have the same data type. This can lead to logic errors if you assume that every element will be of the same type. Instead, all we can assume is that every element will be of type `Object`, and since `Object` is the ultimate base type for *every* type, this could be anything, and so anything can go into an `ArrayList`. The problem is that this is not type safe. Another problem is that value types must be boxed to be loaded into the `ArrayList`, and unboxed to be used. Not to mention, even reference types must be explicitly type cast back to the expected data type.

The release of .NET 2.0 introduced the generically-typed `List<T>`, which eliminated both of these problems.

```
var list = new ArrayList
{
  0, 1, 1, 2, 3, 5, 8, 13, 21, 34, 55, 89, "Something" , "strange", true

};

foreach (object number in list)
{
  Console.WriteLine(number);
}
```

**Listing 4.52:** Looping through an `ArrayList`.

The code in Listing 4.52 compiles and runs, even though it may not make sense and will probably not give the expected result.

`List<T>` is type-safe and more performant, and should replace `ArrayList` in most cases. The switch will generally be fairly straightforward, as in Listing 4.53.

```
var list = new List<int>
{
  0, 1, 1, 2, 3, 5, 8, 13, 21, 34, 55, 89
};

foreach (int number in list)
{
  Console.WriteLine(number);
}
```

**Listing 4.53:** Looping through a strongly typed `List<int>`.

Of course, if you actually wanted to mix and match data types, you would be stuck with `ArrayList`, but that is rarely the case.

For many developers, the greatest appeal was how easily you could add items to the array list. A common pattern using the `List<T>` was as shown in Listing 4.54.

```
private List<string> Tokenize (string data)
{
  var returnValue = new List<string>();
  string[] tokens = data.Split(new char[] { ':' });
  foreach (string item in tokens)
  {
    returnValue.Add(item);
  }
  return returnValue;
}
```

**Listing 4.54:** A common pattern loading items into a generic `List<T>`.

This and similar patterns are very common and very intuitive, but they will also introduce memory problems. Behind the scenes there is still a simple array, and resizing these arrays can be an expensive operation. It is easy to forget about this overhead, but it is still there.

From Reflector, the implementation for the Add method is shown in Listing 4.55.

```
public void Add(T item)
{
  if (this._size == this._items.Length)
  {
    this.EnsureCapacity(this._size + 1);
  }
  this._items[this._size++] = item;
  this._version++;
}
```

**Listing 4.55:** Internal implementation of the Add method.

The dangerous part is the `EnsureCapacity` method shown in Listing 4.56.

```
private void EnsureCapacity(int min)
{
  if (this._items.Length < min)
  {
    int num = (this._items.Length == 0) ? 4
    : (this._items.Length * 2);
    if (num < min)
    {
      num = min;
    }
    this.Capacity = num;
  }
}
```

**Listing 4.56:** The `EnsureCapacity` method means that memory doubles when more is needed.

This method means that if there are no elements in the array, it will initialize it to 4 elements. If there *are* elements in the array but more are needed, we will double the size of the array. Of course, as a user of the List<T>, you are completely oblivious to this doubling, because the resizing logic happens in the Capacity property, which has two significant implications. Firstly, if we do not properly initialize our List, we will need to perform several resizing operations as the size grows. This means that, when you have a small list, you will spend more time resizing arrays than anything else. The second implication is that, with large arrays, we may actually have twice as much memory allocated as we would expect. As soon as you hit one of the power of 2 boundaries, the memory allocated will be doubled, which will cause your program to use more memory than you would expect.

It is important to not accept the default constructor for List and its variations. Instead, use the overloaded constructor where you can specify the initial capacity. This will reduce the number of initial resizing operations that are needed. If you pick the initial size well, you may be able to entirely eliminate the need for resizing operations. Just be careful, because if you guess too low, then as soon as you exceed your estimate the memory requirements of your code will double.

Using overloaded constructors, the Tokenize method that we saw earlier could be rewritten as in Listing 4.57.

```
private List<string> Tokenize(string data)
{
  string[] tokens = data.Split(new char[] { ':' });

  var returnValue = new List<string>(tokens.Count());
  returnValue.AddRange(tokens);
  return returnValue;
}
```

**Listing 4.57:** A memory sensitive optimization of the original Tokenize method.

Or even as in Listing 4.58.

```
private List<string> Tokenize(string data)
{
  string[] tokens = data.Split(new char[] { ':' });
  var returnValue = new List<string>(tokens );
  return returnValue;
}
```

**Listing 4.58:** Another memory sensitive optimization.

Either of these rewrites will result in the internal array being perfectly sized for the data in it.

Be suspicious of any code that does not specify an initial size for any List<T> or ArrayList objects. There is a very good chance that you will be using more memory than you anticipate, and more memory than you should.

# Excessive References

Imagine your application has loaded into memory a complex domain model such as the one shown in Figure 4.8.

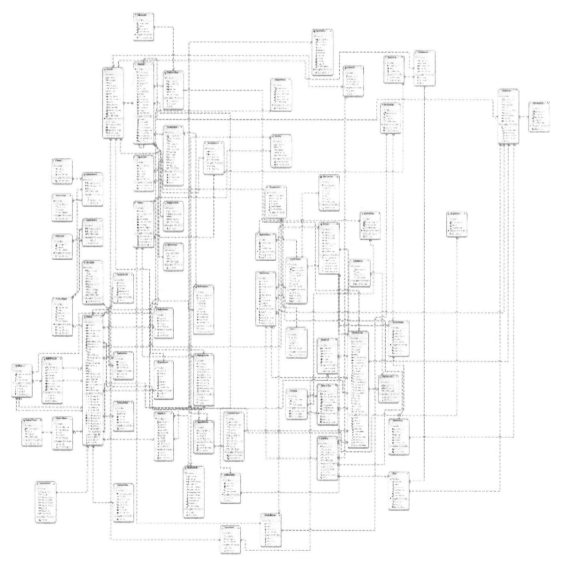

**Figure 4.8:**    A complex domain model.

The GC must obviously analyze the entire graph to discover which objects can be collected. Complex models like that in Figure 4.8 will clearly tax the collector more than simple ones, which affects performance. The solution is to use architectural designs that load information as needed and release it when it is no longer necessary to maintain the reference.

Use `LazyLoading` to delay initializing related properties until they are referenced. For instance, if your domain model refers to a mortgage loan origination system, you may have domain objects related to the `Property` to `Borrowers` to `EmploymentHistory` to `CreditTransactions`, etc. All of which are relevant and necessary for much of your logic, but when you are calculating an amortization schedule, very little of that matters. If you load a loan object into memory to calculate the amortization schedule, you will need to pull out the loan amount, term, interest rate, and monthly payment – you *don't* need to load any details on the borrower or the property. Initializing only what is needed will reduce the complexity of your domain models and lessen the burden on the GC.

# Excessive Writes and Hitting the Write Barrier

Writing to a memory address by modifying an old object causes a range of memory to be flagged as modified. The GC then treats those objects as roots it needs to analyze in order to determine if any objects need to be collected. Older objects aren't typically written to, so this is efficient in many programs. However, if a complex model is stored, as detailed in the previous section, and is modified, it will affect performance by forcing the GC to start tracking more objects.

# Fragmentation

Heap fragmentation occurs when objects are collected from the Large Object Heap and new objects are allocated in the leftover space. If there are pinned objects in the heap, compacting is not performed and gaps are left behind. More to the point, new objects will not fit into the gaps (and are preferentially allocated to the end of the heap anyway), and so the allocated memory expands. In long-running applications with large objects, this can result in `OutOfMemory` exceptions despite the availability of unused memory, because there just isn't a large enough block of memory for an object to fit in. This is typically a Generation 2 / LOH problem (as we discussed in Chapter 2, *The Simple Heap Model*), and it can be detected by comparing free blocks of memory versus the total size of memory.

Some fragmentation will always occur in the life of an application. Avoiding pinning will help avoid this problem. If you're not aware, pinning occurs when using fixed variables or fixed-size buffers. This creates a guaranteed location and size for a variable, which can be passed to an external, unmanaged DLL.

# Long-Lived Objects

Only a full garbage collection will take care of an object that has made it to Gen 2, and thus these objects can possibly consume memory long after they are dead. It is therefore best to make sure that the size of each of these objects is kept to a minimum.

Inefficient code can make objects live longer than they should, reaching Gen 2 and wasting memory unnecessarily. Avoid this by only allocating objects you need, and letting go of references when they're no longer necessary: references on the stack cause rooted objects for the GC. I often review code that has been rewritten several times and has had no attention paid to cleanup. It does not take much time for well-structured code to degenerate into a mess.

Keep your methods small, create objects as close as possible to when you're going to use them, and always remember to call `Dispose()` on your disposable objects. If an object is created before a slow method call and won't be needed after it returns, release the object before calling the method. If the GC runs while this long-running process is running, the object will be promoted to a later generation. Objects take longer to collect.

# Conclusion

As we have seen, memory management touches on every part of the .NET framework; make no mistake, we've covered a good deal of material here. To start with, we've reviewed the Type system and explored the implications of the `Disposable` pattern, and we've also reviewed some of the troubles that you can run into with string manipulation, and the implications of the fact that strings are immutable.

You should now be familiar with the differences between a class and a struct, and how these differences can impact your memory footprint. We've also worked through how to properly implement a struct so that it will be well behaved for hashing, as well as how to avoid some of the potential problems of boxing a struct.

We traced through the history of elevating functions to fully-fledged data types, reviewed the evolution from delegates to anonymous functions to lambdas, and then reviewed closures and how they can extend the lifespan of referenced objects.

We also saw how the new `yield` statement can impact our memory footprint; using this new keyword, we can process a collection of data without having to load the entire collection into memory. This allows us to keep our code well structured, but still take advantage of reduced memory requirements.

Along the way, we saw how handy data structures such as the generic list make it easy to manipulate and process lists of data. This data type is so simple to use that it is easy to forget about what is happening in the background.

We explored some of the implications of not properly initializing the size of the `List` `<T>` with the constructor (if you're not careful, you can potentially have lists that are sized for twice as much data as they actually hold!).

Having made it through this *tour de force* of the .NET framework, we are ready to move on to the next chapter and see how these concepts contribute to some recurring problems in various .NET applications and frameworks. Take a deep breath, and let's jump right back in, in Chapter 5.

# Chapter 5: Application-Specific Problems

## Introduction

A true memory leak is rare; memory hogs are much more common. A memory hog will cause the framework to hold on to more memory than you would anticipate, and looks suspiciously like a memory leak. Regardless of the cause, the symptoms and the pain are the same. Your application may take a performance hit as the system starts paging. You may notice that your application seems to freeze periodically for garbage collection. In the worst-case scenario, your application may crash with `OutOfMemoryExceptions`.

Naturally, different applications share common areas of contention that are often problematic, and we're going take a look at some of the more commonly occurring pitfalls in this chapter. I should make it clear that we are going to skim through a broad range of technologies to give you a sense of where their common pitfalls are, as well as dip into a few unique gotchas which you'll only find in one place. The purpose of this is not to give you an A–Z guide, but rather to give you an appreciation of the .NET memory management landscape, and perhaps give you a few nudges towards areas to watch out for. With that in mind, let's dive right in.

## IIS and ASP.NET

Regardless of whether you use vanilla ASP.NET or MVC, you use IIS to serve up your web pages. Properly configured, IIS can certainly help improve your application throughput but, misconfigured, it can be a major bottleneck. Some of these configuration settings are out of the scope of memory management but, to be honest, *all* settings need to be carefully reviewed to ensure that they are not causing problems.

# Caching

Caching is a broad and subtle art, and so I'm going to devote a fair amount of attention to it. It is common to try and improve application performance with caching. If a page changes rarely, or is expensive to retrieve or calculate, caching can be an easy way to create a more responsive user experience. While this is a common strategy, it is not without risks. If not properly implemented, this clever performance enhancement can easily create more problems than you were trying to solve, as I'm sure you can imagine.

You can easily cache a page in its entirety:

```
<%@ OutputCache Duration="240" VaryByParam="none" %>
```

**Listing 5.1:**    Simple caching.

This means that the page will not be processed again for 240 seconds, and the exact same page will be returned, unchanged, for every request in that timeframe. This can take some load off the web server and make key pages seem more responsive. We have to balance this against the amount of memory that caching will consume. All of this cached memory will ultimately show up in the memory space for the worker process. If we cache too much data, memory usage will grow out of hand, and the web server may spend more time than it should in garbage collections or recycling the web server to reclaim these resources. This is a delicate balance that must be determined for your own application and server configuration.

You may not always be able to cache an entire page. Indeed, caching the whole page would often not make sense. For example, perhaps caching the entire page would take up too much memory, or perhaps there would be too many copies based on the number of potential versions. A more common practice is to cache only parts of the page. You can pull the parts that can be cached into user controls and cache them, while keeping the rest of the page dynamic.

The caching directive has several parameters, of which two are required:

- the `Duration` parameter sets how many seconds the page cache will be retained

- the `VaryByParam` parameter specifies `QueryString` or `postback` variables on which different caches will be served, but the value `"none"` indicates that this is to be ignored.

Other values can be included and separated with semicolons. For example, the `page;count` value indicates that a different cache should be stored for each encountered combination of variables `page` and `count`. However you handle your caching, you want to limit the number of parameters listed and the number of unique combinations specified, otherwise there will be too many copies of the page or control in cache. Trying to cache the paging output for a grid could easily consume all of your memory. Consider a paging scenario where you had 20 pages with 5 potential values for the count variable. In this scenario, there would be 100 copies of the page or control being cached. As you add parameters, multiply the number of potential values for each parameter together, to get the number of potential copies.

Sometimes, instead of a set duration, we might like to refresh a page or control's cache based upon modifications to SQL data. This requires setting up a SQL Cache Dependency, and enabling SQL Server Service Broker on the database. There are a couple of different ways to set up the Service Broker. We will step through one approach in some detail, but if you do not need these details, feel free to skip to the next section.

To start with, exclusive access to the database is necessary to enable the broker.

```
ALTER DATABASE MyDatabase SET SINGLE_USER WITH ROLLBACK IMMEDIATE
ALTER DATABASE MyDatabase SET ENABLE_BROKER
ALTER DATABASE MyDatabase SET MULTI_USER
```

**Listing 5.2:** Setting up access to your SQL database.

We also need to run **aspnet_regsql** to register the database and tables for notification.

```
aspnet_regsql -d MyDatabase -E -S . -ed
aspnet_regsql -d MyDatabase -E -S . -et -t ReferenceTable
```

**Listing 5.3:** Registering the database and tables for notification.

**aspnet_regsql** is a handy tool when it comes to creating key databases used by the membership provider for ASP.NET. It can also be used to add or remove options on an existing database. In this case, we will use it to configure cache dependency options. If you want to know a bit more about how to use it, Table 5.1 summarizes some of the key options.

| | |
|---|---|
| **-d** | The name of the database to act on |
| **-E** | Tells the command to use windows authentication |
| **-S** | The name of the server. "." Means to use the current server |
| **-ed** | Enables SQL cache dependency |
| **-dd** | Disables SQL cache dependency |
| **-et** | Enables SQL cache dependency on a table |
| **-dt** | Disables SQL cache dependency on a table |
| **-t** | Specifies which table to enable caching on |
| **-lt** | Lists the tables that have cache dependency enabled |

**Table 5.1:** The key options for **aspnet_regsql**.

Finally, we need to configure the caching element in the config file (Listing 5.4).

```
<configuration>
  <system.web>
    <compilation debug="false" targetFramework="4.0" />
    <caching>
      <sqlCacheDependency enabled = "true" pollTime = "60000" >
        <databases>
          <add name="ReferenceData"
            connectionStringName="ConnectionString"
            pollTime="6000000" />
        </databases>
      </sqlCacheDependency>
    </caching>
  </system.web>
  <connectionStrings>
    <add name="ConnectionString" connectionString="…"/>
  </connectionStrings>
</configuration>
```

**Listing 5.4:**   Making sure the caching element in the `config` file is correctly set up.

Once everything is configured, we can now include the `SQLDependency` in the `OutputCache` directive (Listing 5.5).

```
<%@ OutputCache Duration="600" VaryByParam="none"
SqlDependency="ReferenceData:ReferenceTable"%>
```

**Listing 5.5:**   Caching based on a database dependency.

This configuration will cause the page or control to be refreshed whenever the data in the `ReferenceTable` is updated.

# Cache limits

We also have various cache limit configuration settings that we need to be aware of. These limits are intended to help ensure that caching does not create memory problems but, if misconfigured, these limits could undermine your caching strategy.

The cache element in the `web.config` file defines the following attributes to help manage the size of your caches. When any of these limits are exceeded, the data in the cache will be trimmed.

| | |
|---|---|
| **privateBytesLimit** | This is the maximum number of bytes that the host process is permitted to consume before the cache is trimmed. This is not the memory dedicated to the cache. This is the total memory usage by the w3wp process (in IIS7). |
| **percentage PhysicalMemory UsedLimit** | This is the maximum percentage of RAM that the machine can use before the cache is trimmed. With 4GB of RAM and this attribute set to 80%, the cache would be trimmed if Task Manager reported over 3.2gb (i.e. 80% of 4GB) was in use. This is not the percentage memory used by ASP.NET or caching; this is the memory used machine-wide. |

**Table 5.2:** Attributes in the cache element of the ASP.NET `web.config` file.

IIS7 provides another configuration point that may complicate matters from a caching perspective. The Private Memory Limit is an advanced property of the App Pool, which defines the maximum number of private bytes a worker process can consume before it is recycled. Among other things, this will clear the cache and reclaim all of the memory used by the worker process. If you set this limit lower than `privateBytesLimit` in `web.config`, you'll always get a recycle before a cache trim. You will probably always want to set this value higher than the `privateBytesLimit` so that trimming of the cache can have a chance to solve memory pressure before recycling the worker process.

Caching can be a great way to make an application more responsive. Used appropriately, caching can solve performance problems, but abusing caching (by not carefully tracking what is being cached) can create a memory hog in even a well-behaved application. When things go wrong, the cache limits can control the damage and prevent your application from running out of memory.

**Figure 5.1:** App Pool configuration for the Private Memory Limit.

# Debug

Inside the `web.config`, there is a critical setting (see Listing 5.6). This is the default setting, but it has an unfortunate side effect from a performance perspective.

```
<compilation debug="true">
```

**Listing 5.6:** Turning on debugging in `web.config`.

This setting will inject debug symbols into the compiled assemblies. It also disables batch compilation, which means that each page will be compiled into separate assemblies. More specifically, each `aspx`, `ascx`, and `asax` will get its own assembly. In many web applications this could easily mean having dozens of assemblies and, as well as being unwieldy, these extra assemblies can also lead to memory fragmentation. Remember that each assembly has its associated metadata, and when you have assemblies with only one class in them, you can easily have more metadata than application data.

As I mentioned a moment ago, each of these assemblies will be compiled with debug symbols, resulting in poorer performance, and meaning that the GC will not work as effectively as in a release build. Essentially, the GC will be less aggressive in reclaiming memory when debug symbols are included. Since the debug symbols are included, the GC needs to be prepared that a debugger could be attached, and many of the rules for identifying unreachable references may not be applicable. With a debugger attached, a lot more objects may be reachable.

So, there is an overhead for each assembly, and since each assembly is compiled in debug mode there is *additional* overhead for the debugging details. But that's not all. Finally, each assembly gets its own block of memory for its metadata, meaning that there will be space between the assemblies. With a large number of assemblies, that means we'll quickly start to see fragmentation within the Virtual Address Space, making it increasingly harder to find large enough spaces to store the managed heaps, which then runs the risk of causing out of memory exceptions.

Even if you have debug set to `false`, you may still end up with multiple assemblies. "Why?" I hear you ask. This is because even with debug set to `false`, edits to a page will result in recompiling that one page into a separate assembly. Fortunately, the framework is prepared for this deployment strategy, and provides the `numRecompiles BeforeAppRestart` configuration setting.

Thus, if you need to update individual pages frequently, you can set the `numRecompiles BeforeAppRestart` attribute in the compilation section of the `web.config` to force an App restart after a certain number of recompiles. This can at least limit the potential damage. Just to give you a quiet sense of foreboding, the default value of this attribute is 15, meaning that you could have 15 extra assemblies before the application recompiles.

As always, test with different values to see what works best with your application. You have to balance the number of assemblies created with how often you are forcing an application restart. Of course, you need to rethink your deployment strategy if it relies on editing deployed pages individually.

# StringBuilder

Every control is built using a `StringBuilder`. The `Render` method accepts an `HTMLTextWriter`, which is backed by a `StringBuilder`, and the contents of the `StringBuilder` are ultimately written back to the client as the HTML that is displayed. The `StringBuilder` is a good choice for string concatenation and offers much better performance than a simple string.

Much like we saw in the previous chapter with the `List`, a `StringBuilder` grows to accommodate the string being built. Internally, the `StringBuilder` uses a string to hold the string being built, and uses an `EnsureCapacity` method to verify that this internal string will hold the string that is being built. This method has the same potential problem that we saw with `List`; namely, that the internal string will double in size every time it has to grow. This will result in lots of intermediate strings being created, which will all be garbage collected, but will also cause your application to spend more time garbage collecting than it should, as a result. When you create the `StringBuilder`, you can explicitly initialize the size of the internal buffer and, as we saw in Chapter 4, *Common Memory Problems*, this can substantially reduce the memory pressure in your application.

Unfortunately, you don't have the option to explicitly create the `StringBuilder`. However, you can limit the potential problems by reducing the number of controls you implement, as well as the amount of HTML needed to render these controls.

# ADO.NET

There are many object-relational model (ORM) solutions available, but there are also plenty of applications with custom data layer implementations using pure ADO.NET. For performance reasons, some designs are meant to directly pull data, skipping the ORM subsystem entirely, but even if you are using an ORM tool, ADO.NET is still relevant. Under the hood of every ORM sits ADO.NET

Many of the classes used in ADO.NET implement the IDisposable interface (which we saw in Chapter 4 when dealing with unmanaged resources), and their lifespans should be limited to prevent resource leakage. ADO.NET deals with many unmanaged components, and so there's some quite straightforward good advice to bear in mind: explicitly wrap Connections, Commands, and Adapters with using statements. Open connections as late as you can, and explicitly close them as soon as you can. The using statement will ensure that the Dispose method is called when the object goes out of the scope of the using block.

```
public DataTable GetData()
{
    using (var connection = new SqlConnection(ConnectionString))
    using (var command = new SqlCommand(storedProcedure, connection))
    using (var adapter = new SqlDataAdapter(command))
    {
        DataTable dataTable = new DataTable("Table");
        adapter.Fill(dataTable);
        return dataTable;
    }
}
```

**Listing 5.7:** Implementations of simple best practices with ADO.NET.

There are also certain objects that should never be used for caching purposes. While caching data can often improve your application performance, nothing from the System.Data namespace should ever be cached. It may seem natural to cache DataTables,

`DataAdapters`, or `DataSets`, (and, indeed, it *can* be done) but these can easily grow out of hand and negate any benefits you might have gained from caching.

These objects are very "heavy," in that they have a lot of extra data and overhead associated with them. Naturally, you should always use the lightest-weight object that you can. Cache data with simple arrays, and populate these arrays with simple objects (ideally these will have simple read/write properties for the fields that are needed). Such objects are often referred to as POCO objects (Plain Old CLR Objects).

# LINQ

LINQ (Language-Integrated Query) makes the promise of allowing you to query objects in memory with the same ease as querying a database. For the most part, LINQ lives up to the hype and, if you are at all familiar with SQL, the syntax for LINQ will feel natural.

Another promise of LINQ is improved memory management but, as with everything we're discussing in this chapter, it may also have the opposite affect and dramatically increase the memory footprint if you're not careful. The improved memory management rests in the potential of delayed execution and having to load entire results lists into memory at the same time. LINQ uses the `yield` statement we saw in Chapter 4 to avoid having to return all of the data until the `IEnumerable<T>` or `IQueryable<T>` is expanded.

LINQ to Objects are extensions built on `IEnumerable<T>` that allow you to query arrays and collection types in memory, and they are implemented in much the same way described in the `yield` section of Chapter 4. The extensions typically take delegates as parameters to be called during the iteration of the `IEnumerable<T>`. Thanks to features such as the `yield` statement, lists can be processed without bringing the whole list into memory at a time. Clearly this means that, depending on your query, your memory footprint may well be reduced.

Other forms of LINQ, such as LINQ to Entity Framework, utilize the `IQueryable<T>` interface. The extensions for this interface take expression trees as parameters and pass them off to the `IQueryProvider`, which is then responsible for interpreting the expression trees to another language, such as T-SQL.

`IQuerytable<T>` defines `IEnumerable<T>` in its contract, which leads to this problem I'm about to describe, and which some developers encounter in their code. Listing 5.8 demonstrates a LINQ to Entity Framework call implemented using the extension method syntax.

```
Order[] pastDueAccounts = null;
DateTime dueDate = DateTime.Today.AddDays(-7);
using (var context = new Context())
{
    pastDueAccounts = context.Accounts
        .Where(account => account.DueDate < dueDate).ToArray();
}
```

**Listing 5.8:** Implementing a LINQ to Entity Framework call.

This code is pulling the past week's orders out of the database. One may be tempted to refactor the lambda expression in the `Where` clause. After all, it does represent a filter, and it is usually a good thing to encapsulate logic that may change or be used in multiple places.

```
public bool PastDueAccount(Account account)
{
    return account.DueDate < DateTime.Today.AddDays(-7);
}
```

**Listing 5.9:** Refactoring the lambda expression.

With such a method, it seems natural to rewrite our original query as:

```
Order[] pastDueAccounts = null;
using (var context = new Context())
{
    pastDueAccounts = context.Accounts
                        .Where(account => PastDueAccount(account))
                        .ToArray();
}
```

**Listing 5.10:** Rewriting the original LINQ to Entity Framework call.

This logic is actually incorrect, but it may not be caught until after an application has been deployed and the database has had time to accumulate data. Let me explain why.

With the original method, the compiler generated an expression tree and the database was queried for a limited amount of data. On the other hand, the refactored example pulls all of the orders from the database and then filters them in memory. The SQL that is generated will actually exclude the filtering restrictions, which will not be interpreted until *after* the SQL is run and the results returned.

Instead of having the filter use indexes in the database and call up a small subset of the data, no indexes will be used, and the entire contents of the table will be retrieved. For as long as the database has a small number of records, this will not cause a problem, but it will quickly cause *substantial* problems as the database volume grows.

Why do we get this behavior? The compiler implicitly converts lambda expressions to either expression trees or delegates, depending on the context in which they are defined, but named methods are not converted to expression trees. They therefore don't match any of the extension methods for `IQueryable<T>`, and are not incorporated into the SQL that is sent to the database. Instead, they are treated as delegates and passed to `IEnumerable<T>`, and the delegate operates on the objects returned from the SQL call.

This problem can be avoided by returning a lambda expression from the `Where` method, meaning we can rewrite our `PastDueAccount` method as shown in Listing 5.11.

```
public Expression<Func<Order, bool>> PastDueAccount
{
    get
    {
        DateTime startDate = DateTime.Today.AddDays(-7);
        return order => order.TransactionDate > startDate;
    }
}
```

**Listing 5.11:** Filtering function implemented as an expression.

This way, the lambda expression will be passed to the LINQ provider, and its logic will be incorporated into the final query.

The difference is subtle. The LINQ provider does not know what to do with a delegate like the first implementation of the `PastDueAccount` method. It only knows how to deal with expression trees, and will ignore the delegate. Once the expression tree is parsed by the LINQ provider and the resultant SQL executed on the database, then `IEnumerable` knows exactly how to deal with the delegate and will parse through the results after the query is run.

The end result will be the exact same data, but your computer, the network, and even the database will have to do substantially more work if you get it wrong.

# Windows Presentation Foundation (WPF)

## Event handlers

Event handlers are a common source of memory leaks in WPF applications and, if not handled properly, they can cause problems in WinForms as well. The problem starts when a method from one class is wired up as the event handler for an event from another class. Let's call these the "listener" and the "source;" the problem happens when the source has a longer lifetime than the listener because, as long as the source is alive and has a reference to the listener, the listener cannot be garbage collected.

This will often happen with related windows such as a master/detail or a parent/child window. It can be a subtle problem with a big impact, and it's easy to overlook until you start having memory issues. Once you start seeing the problem, chances are you will have a substantial amount of cleanup work to catch up on. Your best bet is not to worry about when it can lead to problems, and instead always code defensively to avoid the problem in the first place.

A common UI design uses a master/detail relationship. You may have a grid with a list of master records, and when you click on a record from the master grid, a new window opens with the details associated with that master record. If the master window wires up events in the detail window, then the detail window cannot be garbage collected until the event handlers in the master window release their references to the detail window. In this case, the detail window will be the listener and the master window is the source. In most cases, the master window will outlive the details window, but if the event handlers are not handled properly, then the detail window cannot be garbage collected as long as the master window is alive.

```
Detail.SomeEvent += new EventHandler(Master.SomeEvent_Handler);
```

**Listing 5.12:** Registering an event handler.

In this example, `Detail` will not be collected as long as `Master` is still wired as an Event Handler. The easiest way to avoid this problem is to explicitly remove the event handlers when you are through with the object.

```
Detail.SomeEvent -= new EventHandler(Master.SomeEvent_Handler);
```

**Listing 5.13:** Removing an event handler.

Removing the event handlers is easy enough. *Remembering* to do this is the problem.

Another potential pitfall is wiring up events to methods defined in a static class. The problem is that the static class will always be in memory, so the class with the events wired up to the static method will not be garbage collected until the reference is explicitly removed. Again, the fix is to explicitly remove the event handlers.

In general, be wary of static event handlers; even though there would only ever be a single instance of one, it is *always* reachable, as is any class that it is wired up to.

With some of the new language constructs in C# 3.0, a common trend has been to replace the event handler with a lambda expression. Depending on your sense of style, this makes the code easier to read and keeps your class from being cluttered with simple one-line methods that are only used for event handling. Some people may mistakenly believe that this provides a solution to unwiring an event handler, since only a lambda expression is used. However, consider the example in Listing 5.14.

```
public Form()
{
    InitializeComponent();
    button.Click += (sender, e) => MessageBox.Show("Under the Hood");
}
```

**Listing 5.14:** Event handler implemented in a lambda expression.

Looking at this code in .NET Reflector without any optimizations, we see that the compiler generates a delegate to be wired up as the event handler (Listing 5.15).

```
[CompilerGenerated]
private static void <.ctor>b__0(object sender, EventArgs e)
{
    MessageBox.Show("Under the Hood");
}

public Form1()
{
    this.components = null;
    this.InitializeComponent();
    this.button.Click +=
            ((CS$<>9__CachedAnonymousMethodDelegate1 != null)
            ? CS$<>9__CachedAnonymousMethodDelegate1
            : (CS$<>9__CachedAnonymousMethodDelegate1 =
            new EventHandler(Form1.<.ctor>b__0)));
}

[CompilerGenerated]
private static EventHandler CS$<>9__CachedAnonymousMethodDelegate1;
```

**Listing 5.15:** What the compiler produces to deal with a lambda expression as an event handler.

This approach will actually backfire. Not only do you still get the delegate but, because it is anonymous and compiler generated, you don't have a reference to unwire it, which is still a necessary process. Therefore, if you want to use lambda expressions, make sure that you save a reference to the lambda first, so that you can explicitly remove the event handler as needed!

**167**

```
private readonly EventHandler _buttonClickHandler;
public Form1()
{
    InitializeComponent();
    _buttonClickHandler = (sender, e) =>
            MessageBox.Show("under the hood");
    button.Click += _buttonClickHandler;
}
```

**Listing 5.16:** Saving the lambda expression so that we can later unregister it.

Now you have a handy reference to the lambda that can be removed as needed.

```
button.Click -= _buttonClickHandler;
```

**Listing 5.17:** Unregistering the saved lambda expression.

# Weak event pattern

As we previously discussed, it is important to always remove event handlers when they are no longer needed. Not doing so will lead to objects not being eligible for garbage collection for longer than they should be, which will then cause your application to use more memory than it should. So far, all of this should be obvious. Unfortunately, it is *not* always obvious when it is safe to remove the event handler, and this is where weak events come into play.

The weak event pattern is a new design pattern introduced with WPF, designed specifically to solve this problem. This pattern will be used primarily by control designers, particularly when users of the control need to wire up to an event but either cannot easily remove the wired-up event handler, or don't know when to do so.

Weak events work by separating the source from the listener and, in the middle, we place a `WeakEventManager`. In general, you will have a `WeakEventManager` for every "weak" event that you want to expose.

When you want to employ this pattern, you start by deriving a class from `WeakEvent-Manager`, which requires you to complete six steps.

1. Provide a static `AddListener` method.

2. Provide a static `RemoveListener` method.

3. Override the `StartListening` method.

4. Override the `StopListening` method.

5. Implement the `DeliverEvent.`

6. Implement the `CurrentManager` property.

This might look like a lot, but it really isn't. That said, the downside is that you will generally need a `WeakEventManager` for every event that you want a weak event reference to. With *that* said, the upside is that you can have such a relationship with any class, even if it was not designed with weak events in mind.

A typical implementation can be as simple as the one shown in Listing 5.18.

```
protected override void StartListening(object source)
{
    var  button = source as Button ;
    if (button != null)
    {
        button.Click +=  ButtonClick;

    }

}
```

```
protected override void StopListening(object source)
{
    var button = source as Button;
    if (button != null)
    {
        button.Click -= ButtonClick;

    }
}
```

**Listing 5.18:** Basics for implementing the `StartListening` and `StopListening` methods.

The `StartListening` and `StopListening` methods look like a generalized wiring and unwiring of the event handlers, and that's exactly all that is going on. The next thing we have to worry about is the event handler that the manager will provide (Listing 5.19).

```
void ButtonClick(object sender, EventArgs e)
{
    DeliverEvent(sender, e);
}
```

**Listing 5.19:** The humble `ButtonClick` method.

Most of the time, this event handler will look the same; we are simply forwarding the event to everyone who expressed an interest in it. The only real difference from one implementation to the next will be the method signature, as it *must* match the signature of the method being managed.

Now we can move on to the mechanics of allowing relevant listeners to express their interest in these events (Listing 5.20).

```
public static void AddListener(Button source,
            IWeakEventListener listener)
{
    CurrentManager.ProtectedAddListener(source, listener);
}
```

```
public static void RemoveListener(Button source,
              IWeakEventListener listener)
{
    CurrentManager.ProtectedRemoveListener(source, listener);
}
```

Listing 5.20: The basics of implementing the AddListener and RemoveListener.

You may notice that both methods are expecting the object that will be raising the events *and* an object implementing the IWeakEventListener interface. We will deal with this interface shortly but, for now, just know that this is a simple interface that any object listening for weak events needs to implement. These two methods will probably look very similar to this in most implementations, with only the data type of the first parameter changing.

You'll also notice that both of these methods refer to a CurrentManager, which is a simple static property that you are responsible for implementing. The implementation shown in Listing 5.21 ensures that only a single instance is used, and handles initializing this instance if it is not already initialized.

```
private static ButtonClickEventManager CurrentManager
{
    get
    {
        var managerType = typeof(ButtonClickEventManager);
        var manager =  GetCurrentManager(managerType)
            as ButtonClickEventManager;
        if (manager == null)
        {
            manager = new ButtonClickEventManager();
            SetCurrentManager(managerType, manager);
        }
        return manager;
    }
}
```

Listing 5.21: Manager's implementation of the CurrentManager method.

With this plumbing out of the way, we are ready to turn our attention to the `IWeakListener` interface that we saw earlier.

Any object that wants to receive weak events needs to implement the `IWeakListener` interface and then be passed to the `WeakEventManager`'s `AddListener` method. The interface has a very simple definition; it just requires a single method `ReceiveWeakEvent`.

A common implementation may look similar to the one in Listing 5.22.

```
public Boolean ReceiveWeakEvent(Type managerType,
        Object sender, EventArgs e)
{
    if (managerType == typeof(ButtonClickEventManager))
    {
        OnButtonClick(sender, e );
        return true;
    }
    else
    {
        return false;

    }
}
```

Listing 5.22: A simple implementation of the `ReceiveWeakEvent` method.

The type parameter will tell you which event manager delivered the event, which will tell you which event was raised. Return `true` if you were able to respond to the event, or `false` if you were not expecting the event.

If multiple buttons are being listened to, you can use the sender parameter to tell you which one raised the event. Alternatively, if multiple events are being monitored, you can use the `managerType` parameter to identify which event was raised. Even if you are interested in multiple events from multiple objects, you need only a single `Receive-WeakEvent` method.

This has been a fairly lengthy discussion (in relation to the rest of this chapter), but hopefully you can see that, once properly laid out, the weak event pattern is fairly straightforward to implement, and does effectively eliminate the problem of the listener staying alive longer than expected.

# Command bindings

Command bindings were introduced with Silverlight 4. They create strong references and may have the same issues as event handlers.

A command is a piece of logic or, more precisely, an object implementing the ICommand interface. This interface requires two methods and an event handler. The methods are CanExecute and Execute, and the event is CanExecuteChanged. The CommandBinding is the object that maps the command logic to the command, and it also hosts the event handlers. The Command object is responsible for determining whether or not a command is valid.

Consider the example in Listing 5.23.

```
private void commandButton_Click(object sender, RoutedEventArgs e)
{
    var child = new ChildWindow();
    var  command = new RoutedCommand();
    command.InputGestures.Add(new KeyGesture(Key.Escape));
    child.CommandBindings.Add(
            new CommandBinding(command, CloseWindow));
    child.Show();
}

private void CloseWindow(object sender, ExecutedRoutedEventArgs e)
{
    var window = sender as Window;
```

```
    if (window != null)
    {
        window.Close();
    }
}
```

**Listing 5.23:**  Properly releasing an event handler after it is no longer needed.

In this example, a reference will be held in each child window, and the main window cannot be collected until all child windows with this command are ready for collection or have removed the command. Just as with event handlers, you need to explicitly remove the command.

A good practice is to clear all of the binding information when you are through with the child. From within the context of the child window, you can easily clear this binding information (Listing 5.24).

```
BindingOperations.ClearAllBindings(this);
```

**Listing 5.24:**  Clearing all bindings including the command bindings.

This simple strategy will ensure that command bindings do not prevent your objects from being eligible for collection as soon as possible.

# Data binding

The data binding system in WPF was built so that it is easy to bind to any kind of object, convert values to an appropriate representation, and update the binding in case the object is changed. It does all this while trying to ensure that references are not maintained, or are at least weak, so that garbage collection can be performed at the appropriate time. There is a great deal of work done behind the scenes to simplify data binding and make type conversions straightforward.

WPF also sets the lofty goal of minimizing the likelihood of data binding creating memory leaks. Among other things, WPF wants to make it simple and straightforward to bind data to the UI.

```
control.ItemsSource = collection;
```

**Listing 5.25:** Simple data binding.

If the control in question is an `ItemControl` and the collection implements `INotifyCollectionChanged`, then the item control will automatically wire up to the collection's `CollectionChanged` event. This is both powerful and dangerous, as "easy" does not always also mean "sensible."

For all that WPF takes a lot of complexity away from tired eyes, I hope you can see why it's worth being aware that that complexity still exists, and still needs to be factored into your code.

# Windows Communication Framework

Windows Communication Framework (WCF) is Microsoft's solution for distributed computing and Service-Oriented Applications (SOA). With WCF you can spread the processing load over one or more servers, allowing you to put the presentation logic on one server and the data access / business logic on another. There are a couple of issues inherent in such a separation, but there are also some compelling reasons to follow this type of deployment model.

# Benefits

You may want to use this to better support connection pooling to the database, which is especially useful with desktop applications.

You may want to do this to improve security, such that only the data servers need to be able to connect to the database, and the presentation servers can be blocked. This is especially useful with Internet-facing applications, where the presentation servers are in the Demilitarized Zone (DMZ), and everything else is safely behind the firewalls.

You may want to do this to lower the cost of initializing an ORM system. Initializing an ORM such as Entity Framework or NHibernate can be expensive, and initializing all of the mapping/configuration information on the data server can lower the cost of starting up the presentation server. Instead of having to load the metadata for every page request, or even in the application start, you can load the metadata when the WCF host is started.

Finally, you may want to do this to help solve bandwidth concerns; in some settings, you may find that the data passed back and forth between the database and the data server is more than the data passed back and forth between the data server and the presentation servers. With web applications, this may not be a major concern because they may well both be on the same network segment, and so the net effect is negligible. But with a desktop application, the database-to-data-server link may be a local network hop, while the data-server-to-presentation link may be a slow network hop over a lower bandwidth.

# Drawbacks

The most obvious drawback is that method calls must now be marshaled across server boundaries. This may mean that something that *looks* like a simple method will actually be an expensive service method call. Essentially, we want to get all of the data we need in as few calls as possible, which also means we want to avoid a "chatty" interface.

Suppose you have a UI screen that needs information from one particular business entity, as well as a collection of other related business entities. Instead of making a call to retrieve the `User` object, and a separate call to retrieve the list of `Permission` objects, you want to retrieve all of this information with one call. Depending on the pattern you are following, this may be known as a **composite DTO (Data Transfer Object)**, or it may be known as `ViewModel`, or you may have your own name for it. The important thing is to reduce the number of service calls.

```
public interface IService
{
    User GetUser(int userId);
    IList<Permission> GetPermissionsByUserId(int userId);
}
```

**Listing 5.26:** A simple "chatty" service interface.

```
public class UserPermissions : CompositeDtoBase
{
    public IList<Permission> Permissions { get; set; }
    public User User { get; set; }
}
```

**Listing 5.27:** A simple composite DTO.

```
public interface IConsolidatedService
{
    UserPermissions GetUserPermissions(int userId);
}
```

**Listing 5.28:** A more streamlined service interface.

# Disposable

The objects in the WCF namespace implement the `IDisposable` interface but, unfortunately, it is not implemented properly. Unlike with other objects that implement the disposable pattern, you should avoid the `Using` statement with a service proxy. If you *do* try it, then the `Dispose()` method of a proxy will call the `Close()` method, which will cause an exception if a fault has occurred on a channel.

Relying on the `Using` construct may also result in orphaned service clients and unmanaged resources. The best practice for properly managing and cleaning up service clients is to follow a pattern similar to the one in Listing 5.29.

```
var clientproxy = new UnderTheHoodClient();
try
{
    clientproxy.Method();
    clientProxy.Close();
}
catch(CommunicationException)
{
    clientProxy.Abort();
}
catch (TimeoutException)
{
    clientProxy.Abort();
}
```

**Listing 5.29:** WCF call pattern.

You can also simplify this into a single method accepting a lambda statement. A `UseAndClose` method will run the action that you specify, and also properly handle the closing of the connection.

```
public static RETURN UseAndCloseService<SERVICE, RETURN>
        (Func<SERVICE, RETURN> block) where SERVICE : class,
                    ICommunicationObject, new()
{
    SERVICE service = null;
    try
    {
        service = new SERVICE();
        return block.Invoke(service);
    }
    finally
    {
        if (service != null)
            CloseWCFService(service);
    }
}
```

**Listing 5.30:** A simple implementation of the UseAndClose method.

In this implementation, we create the service, call the specified method, and then immediately close it. In this example, SERVICE and RETURN are generic type parameters. We pass these two data types in when we make the method call. This allows us to specify the data type for the service but also the return type for the method that we will call. The CloseWCFService may look similar to that in Listing 5.31.

```
public static void CloseWCFService(ICommunicationObject wcfService)
{
    bool success = false;
    if (wcfService != null)
    {
        try
        {
            if (wcfService.State != CommunicationState.Faulted)
            {
                wcfService.Close();
                success = true;
            }
        }
    }
```

```
        catch (Exception ex)
        {
                // log with error
        }
        finally
        {
            if (!success)
                wcfService.Abort();
            wcfService = null;
        }
    }
}
```

**Listing 5.31:** A centralized `CloseService` method.

Using such a method is also relatively straightforward, and you don't even have to sacrifice Intellisense (Listing 5.32).

```
var result = Utility.UseAndCloseService<WcfServiceClient,
        PageResponseDto>(srv => srv.DoWork(param1, param2));
```

**Listing 5.32:** Using the `UseAndCloseService` method.

# Configuration

WCF provides several configuration settings that can influence availability and scalability. The configuration settings can also ultimately influence the resources used under load.

For example, the `serviceThrottling` element has three attributes (see Table 5.3). There is no magic combination that should be used. You need to test your settings under your own load to determine which combination yields the best throughput.

| | |
|---|---|
| `maxConcurrent Calls` | This is a positive integer that determines the maximum number of messages that can be processed concurrently. The default value is 16 times the number of processors on the server, meaning that if there are more than 32 requests on a dual processor server, the extras will be queued up. This also helps prevent the server from being flooded with requests during a usage spike or a DOS attack. If you find that you have a lot of requests queuing up and creating delays in the presentation servers, but resources are not maxed out on the data server, you may want to consider raising this limit. |
| `maxConcurrent Instances` | This is a positive integer that specifies the maximum number of `InstanceContext` objects in the service. This value is influenced by the `InstanceContextMode` attribute: **PerSession** – this value will determine the total number of sessions **PerCall** – this value will determine the total number of concurrent calls **Single** – this value is irrelevant since only one `InstanceContext` will ever be used. Once this threshold is reached, new requests will be queued until an instance context is closed. The default is the sum of the default value of `MaxConcurrentSessions` and the default value of `MaxConcurrentCalls`. |
| `maxConcurrent Sessions` | This is a positive integer that specifies the maximum number of sessions a `ServiceHost` object can accept. The service will accept more requests, but they will not be read until the current number of active sessions fall below this threshold. The default value is 100 times the number of processors. |

**Table 5.3:** `serviceThrottling` attributes and their descriptions.

# Conclusion

We have seen some recurring themes across a wide range of .NET platforms. New technologies often solve old problems, but they often create their own new problems, as well as their own variations on some old problems. Understanding how these problems show up on these various platforms makes it easier to understand and appreciate what new versions and new platforms you should bring to the mix when developing your applications. This makes it easier to learn new technologies and to appreciate where the gotchas are before you get burned.

A few of key areas to always be on the lookout for are:

- not having a properly balanced caching strategy

- abusing a new technique by not applying (or, indeed, understanding) it properly

- unintended references through delegates

- always properly dispose of objects that implement the `IDisposable` interface.

Regardless of the platform being used, these guidelines will serve you well.

# Section 3:
# Deeper .NET

# Chapter 6: A Few More Advanced Topics

## Introduction

We now turn our attention to a couple of more advanced topics. In this chapter, we will explore some of the differences between 32-bit and 64-bit applications from a memory perspective, and we'll see how this affects the size of our objects and what that means to our memory footprint. We will also review some recent changes to the way the CLR deals with memory when the memory caps are lifted.

We'll look at the evolution of the garbage collector (GC), and how problems in each version led to the changes in the next. We have several versions and variations of the .NET framework (and its accompanying GC) to choose from, so we'll review guidelines to help you make the right choice for your application.

One of the most exciting new features introduced in version 4.0 of the framework is Garbage Collection Notifications, and we'll step through how to set up notifications, as well as exploring some potential applications. This is a very new concept, and best applications are still coming to light, so expect this information to evolve in the future.

Finally, we'll turn our attention to marshaling and some of the memory challenges introduced when manipulating unmanaged memory.

# 32-Bit vs. 64-Bit

I remember being asked in philosophy class, "If the world and everything in it suddenly doubled in size, would you notice?" This was a thought experiment with no real answer, and no real implication; it was intended to help you think critically.

With software development, this takes on new significance. This essentially does happen and, in this particular case, we *do* notice. The first, most obvious difference is the effect on memory resource limits. A 32-bit application is capped (without going into deeper details) at 2 GB of Virtual Address Space, whereas a 64-bit application is capped at 8 TB. This is a substantial difference, and sounds like a limit that we are not likely to reach any time soon, but bear in mind that it wasn't too long ago that 2 GB sounded like a ridiculous amount of memory.

Of course, not everything has doubled in size, which is the source of most interoperability issues, and one of the reasons why the change up to 64-bit systems is so noticeable. Pointers and references have doubled in size; other data types have not.

Let's start with the basics and then work our way in. Any given program compiled as a 64-bit application will use more memory than the 32-bit version of the same program. In fact, you will use more than twice the memory, and there are a couple of reasons for this. As we have just seen, the size of a reference has doubled, and the size of a pointer has doubled, which means that, among other things, the metadata for any given object has doubled. On a 32-bit system, each object includes an 8-byte header; on a 64-bit system, these objects will include a 16-byte header.

The size of the header is important, because it is this that led to the recommendations for the smallest possible size of an object. It also means that, if the actual data in a class takes up less space than this header, then that class should be a struct, instead. Otherwise, it will feel like your program is thrashing when your objects use more memory for the *header* than for the actual data. So, because not everything doubles in size when switching from 32-bit architecture to 64-bit architecture, you may want to switch some objects from classes to structs to make the most effective use of memory.

However, bear in mind that this tactic may backfire if you are forced to box and unbox the new structs. Generics will help avoid boxing (as mentioned in Chapter 4, *Common Memory Problems*), but you must be careful. Also, remember the guideline that structs must be immutable; if you cannot follow the guidelines for structs, or if these changes obscure your underlying business logic, then you should carefully weigh the pros and cons for your application.

There are naturally other factors that will lead to your application using more memory; for starters, the actual size of your modules will be increased. For example, `mscorwks.dll` is about 5 MB on x86, 10 MB on x64, and 20 MB on ia64. Also, the CLR itself becomes less frugal with memory than it was with 32 bits (because it can afford to be). Instead, more attention is paid to other optimizations that will have more of an impact. You can clearly see this by investigating the segment size. If you run this `windb` command on a memory dump: `! SOS.eeheap —gc`, you will notice dramatically larger segments (if you're not familiar with it, this command summarizes heap sizes). Don't worry about how much bigger the segments are – this is just an exercise to demonstrate my point. Microsoft is rather tight-lipped on the actual size, and you should not make any design decisions based on what you see, since they reserve the right to change it in the future.

Another point to bear in mind – the Large Object Heap does not change. The size threshold is the same for 64 bits as it was for 32 bits and, since your objects will be bigger in a 64-bit environment, this means that you may have objects winding up in the LOH that were normally placed in the SOH when everything was 32 bit.

The CLR takes advantage of the larger memory limits by raising the thresholds that will trigger garbage collections which, in turn, means that your application will go through fewer garbage collection cycles, although each cycle may take longer. As a result, more memory may be tied up in collectable objects before the system gets around to collecting them.

All of this means that your memory footprint will go up much more than you might expect and, instead of getting an `OutOfMemoryException`, your application may run along happily until all of your system resources are used.

There are a few actions that will be faster in a 64-bit application but, in general, most tasks will actually be *slower*. This is because, while manipulating memory in QWORDS (64-bit blocks, or quad-words) instead of DWORDS (32-bit blocks, or double-words) is faster, this difference is generally absorbed by new costs. The real advantage you get is in having more memory to work with. As mentioned a moment ago, this will naturally lead to fewer garbage collections. Fewer garbage collections will then mean that your code will not be interrupted and brought to safe points as often, which is an immense performance benefit.

# Survey of Garbage Collection Flavors

Depending on your perspective, the GC is either the best feature in the .NET framework, or the bane of modern application development. Throughout the various .NET versions, we have received multiple implementations, each trying to improve on earlier ones, and thereby subtly changing the rules.

In the beginning, there were just two flavors: **Server** and **Workstation** (renamed to Concurrent GC at some stage, but we'll stick with "Workstation" for now). Workstation GC is the default and is the only option available on a single processor computer, and Server GC is available whenever you have more than one processor in the machine. As has been touched upon in Chapter 4, Server GC is optimized for throughput, meaning you get a GC thread for each available processor, each of which runs in parallel.

There are several key points to consider when deciding between Server and Workstation garbage collection. The main thing to bear in mind is that Workstation GC favors responsiveness and Server GC favors throughput: you get fewer things done over a long period of time with Workstation GC, but the application will respond more quickly to any individual action.

Workstation GC runs on the same thread that triggered the garbage collection. This thread will typically run at normal priority, and must compete with all the other running threads for processing time. Since this thread is running at normal priority, it will easily be preempted by the other threads that the operating system is running. This can mean that garbage collecting takes longer than if it had a dedicated thread that was set at a higher priority. On the other hand, Server GC uses multiple threads, each running at the highest priority, making it significantly faster than Workstation GC.

However, Server GC can be resource intensive. With Server GC, a separate high priority thread is spawned for each processor. Each of these threads will be given the highest priority, so they will finish substantially faster than under a workstation equivalent, but they will also preempt all other threads, so all that speed is not free. Consider a web server with 4 processors, and running 4 web applications. If all of these web applications are configured to run with Server GC, there will be 16 threads running at the highest priority, all dedicated to garbage collection.

This leads to the "freeze" that is often experienced during garbage collection in server mode. As the number of processors or the number of applications is increased, the number of threads involved can lead to excessive time context switching, which may affect overall performance. In extreme circumstances, the extra threads created by the Server mode GC may have the opposite effect and degrade performance. Thus, if you are running multiple applications on the same computer or have a shared hosted web server, you *may* want to consider Workstation GC over Server GC. I stress "may," because this *does* go against conventional wisdom and will not necessarily be the correct choice in all scenarios.

Every environment is different. You need to test and profile your application under load, and repeat these tests as your configuration or your load profile changes. Upgrading the number of processors on a server may change the ideal configuration. Adding a new instance of the application, may change the recommendation. Repeatedly testing your application is the only way to truly understand the implications of any changes you may make, and profiling tools (such as the previously mentioned ANTS Memory Profiler and its performance profiling counterpart) can make this process a relatively painless addition to your workflow.

In most cases, you will probably want to use Server GC whenever you are running server processes on a server OS but, on the high end of scaling, this may not always be the case. Essentially, while Server GC is faster than Workstation GC on the same size heap, there can be problems if you're running hundreds of instances of an app because of excessive context switching between threads

Added to this mix, we have **Concurrent GC**, which splits the garbage collection process in two and handles the two cases differently. Concurrent GC is available only under Workstation mode. Generation 0 and 1 collections are handled normally, since they will typically finish quickly anyway, but Generation 2 GCs are handled a little differently. This is where the concurrent part comes into play because, to a certain extent, your program can continue running while the Generation 2 garbage is collected.

Without Concurrent GC, all threads in your application are blocked until the garbage collection is complete. The concurrent part comes into play by allowing your code to continue executing during the Generation 2 GC, albeit within certain strict limitations. Your program can continue running *until* the active thread's ephemeral segment is full (the ephemeral segment is the segment that was most recently allocated by the GC). When you run out of room on this segment, you will be back to being completely blocked until garbage collection is finished.

While the total time to run garbage collection will be longer in Concurrent mode, the amount of lag time or halted processing will be reduced, from a user's perspective. In fact, for a large portion of the time, you may not be blocked at all. The default is to enable Concurrent GC whenever you are running under Workstation mode. However, if you explicitly switch from Server mode to Workstation mode as mentioned earlier (in a shared hosting environment), you should also explicitly disable Concurrent GC. With that in mind, you can easily disable/enable Concurrent GC in the `config` file, as in Listing 6.1.

```
<configuration>
  <runtime>
    <gcConcurrent enabled="true" />
  </runtime>
</configuration>
```

**Listing 6.1:** Configuration settings to enable/disable Concurrent GC.

Concurrent GC is intended to minimize screen freezes during garbage collection and is best suited to application scenarios where a responsive UI is the most critical design goal. Unless you are running a server process on a server OS, you will want to keep Concurrent GC enabled.

.NET 4.0 introduced a new flavor to the table: **Background GC**. Technically this isn't really a new option, as it replaces Concurrent GC, although there have been improvements. In particular, Background GC works just like Concurrent GC *except* that your application isn't blocked when the ephemeral segment is full. Instead we can run a foreground Generation 0 and Generation 1 collection against the ephemeral segment. While this happens, instead of blocking the foreground threads because we are garbage collecting, the background thread running the garbage collection is suspended until the foreground is finished. Because this is strictly a Generation 0 and Generation 1 collection against a single segment, this collection will be very fast. This further reduces the latency on the foreground threads.

There are no new configuration settings for Background GC, so when you target the 4.0 version of the framework and enable Concurrent GC, you will get Background GC.

# Garbage Collection Notification

.NET 4.0 introduced the new concept of Garbage Collection Notification; this allows you to receive notifications just before the system collects garbage, as well as when the collection is completed successfully. Why you might want to do this may not be immediately obvious, but this *does* open up some useful options.

You may want to suspend a resource-intensive operation while the garbage is being collected. This may speed up garbage collection, especially if this is a background process that won't affect the UI.

You may want to flag the load balancer to skip a particular server during garbage collection. This will also speed up garbage collection, while forcing users to the server that will be more responsive.

You may want to explicitly remove data from Session when it becomes obvious that resources are being stressed. Depending on your specific application, it may be possible to delay eventual garbage collection, or streamline the process by explicitly removing objects from Session or Web Cache.

However you use it, this is a new feature and, without a doubt, we will see exciting new applications as we get more familiar with it.

So how do we make this magic work? This actually takes several steps to implement, but they are not difficult steps. Garbage Collection Notification sounds like an event, and you might expect it to follow the normal event wire-up mechanism, but it doesn't. At first, this may sound counter-intuitive, but there is actually a good reason for creating a new notification workflow. You may recall from earlier that poorly controlled event handlers are a common source of memory leaks. That means that, if notifications were implemented as a traditional event off of the GC, you would be guaranteed a memory leak. The code handling the notification would never be flagged as being eligible for collection because the GC, which never goes out of scope, would have a reference to it until the event handler was explicitly removed. The notification process developed for Garbage Collection Notification makes this much more explicit.

Instead, we start by calling `GC.RegisterForFullGCNotification`, and, when we are no longer interested in being notified, we explicitly call `GC.CancelFullGCNotification`. In the middle, we setup a thread to continuously call `GC.WaitForFullGCApproach` and `GC.WaitForFullGCComplete`; and these two methods will return a value from the `GCNotificationStatus` enumeration, which has the potential values shown in Table 6.1.

| | |
|---|---|
| `Succeeded` | The notification is ready to be raised. |
| `Failed` | The notification failed for some reason. |
| `Canceled` | The notification was canceled by calling `CancelFullGCNotification`. |
| `Timeout` | The timeout specified as a parameter to the `wait` methods has passed. |
| `NotApplicable` | This result will generally mean that notification was not registered or Concurrent GC is enabled. |

**Table 6.1:** The possible values for the `GCNotificationStatus`.

We set up monitoring with code like this (Listing 6.2).

```
GC.RegisterForFullGCNotification(30, 30);
var notificationThread = new Thread(WaitForFullGcProc);
notificationThread.Start();
// Application logic that needs to be
// notified about garbage collections
GC.CancelFullGCNotification();
```

**Listing 6.2:** Registering for GC notification.

You may be wondering about the magic constants in the call to `RegisterForFullGC Notification`. This method takes two parameters, `maxGenerationThreshold` and `largeObjectHeapThreshold`. Both parameters can be integers between 1 and 99. Larger values for these parameters will cause the notification to be raised earlier, and smaller values will cause the notification to be raised closer to when the event actually takes place.

The first parameter allows you to specify that you want to be notified based on the number of objects that have survived to Generation 2, and the second parameter specifies that you want to be notified based on the size of the Large Object Heap. However, neither parameter specifies an absolute value, so passing in 30 for the `maxGenerationThreshold` does not imply triggering a Notification when there are 30 objects in Generation 2; it simply means that you want to be notified earlier than if you had passed in a value of 10. Unless you are specifically more interested in one trigger over the other, you may want to pass in the same value for each parameter, as this will help ensure that you are notified at the same stage, regardless of the trigger.

A larger value will give you more time to deal with memory pressure, but you just need to be careful not to set it too high. The higher you set the thresholds, the quicker you get notified but the longer you have to wait on the GC. Play with these parameters in your application to see what works best for your load and the types of objects consuming your memory.

In its simplest form, the `WaitForFullGcProc` may look as in Listing 6.3.

```
public static void WaitForFullGcProc()
{
  while (true)
  {
    var status = GC.WaitForFullGCApproach();
    InterpretNotificationStatus(status,
        "Full notifications");
    // Check for a notification of a completed collection.
    status = GC.WaitForFullGCComplete();
    InterpretNotificationStatus(status,
```

```
            "Full notifications complete");
        Thread.Sleep(500);
    }
}
```

**Listing 6.3:** Simple implementation of a `WaitForFullGC`.

And Listing 6.4 shows how `InterpretNotificationStatus` might look.

```
private static void InterpretNotificationStatus
    (GCNotificationStatus status, string whichOne)
{
    switch (status)
    {
        case GCNotificationStatus.Succeeded:
        {
            Console.WriteLine(whichOne + " raised.");
            break;
        }
        case GCNotificationStatus.Canceled:
        {
            Console.WriteLine(whichOne + " canceled.");
            break;
        }
        case GCNotificationStatus.Timeout:
        {
            Console.WriteLine(whichOne
                + " notification timed out.");
            break;
        }
        case GCNotificationStatus.NotApplicable:
        {
            Console.WriteLine("not applicable.");
            break;
        }
    }
}
```

**Listing 6.4:** A simple implementation showing how to interpret the notification status.

Here, we are simply writing out to the console what notification we are receiving. You can take whatever actions are appropriate in your situation in the individual case statements.

# Weak References

Weak references have been around since the beginning days of the .NET Framework, but they are still not very well known or understood. In a nutshell, weak references allow you to violate some of the fundamental concepts of the GC. A weak reference allows you to flag to the GC that it is OK to collect an object but still keep access to the data through a `WeakReference` object.

If the only reference to a block of memory is a weak reference, then this memory is eligible for garbage collection. When you need to reference the memory again, you can access the `Target` property of the weak reference. If the `Target` is null, then the object has been collected and will need to be re-created. However, if the `Target` is not null, then you can cast it back to the original type, and you are back to having a strong reference to the memory in question.

Obviously, great care should be taken with weak references. You have to carefully check to ensure that the object wasn't collected and re-create as needed. This is also not a good candidate solution for every memory issue. For example, if your memory issue stems from lots of small objects, you may exacerbate the problem, since the weak reference will require more memory than the original reference. Also, if the data is time-consuming to produce or calculate, you may just create more performance problems. If the data in the object is expensive to produce or time sensitive, a weak reference may make matters worse. Just for clarity, if you have to make an external service call to get the data, it is expensive to produce. If you have to use a slow or unreliable network connection, it is expensive to produce, or if the data depends on geo-tagging details, it may be expensive to produce.

The ideal candidate for a weak reference will be easy to calculate and will take up a substantial amount of memory. Naturally, defining "easy to calculate" and "substantial amount of memory" is very application/hardware specific, so let's rather say that the ideal candidate is something that you only want to have one copy of in your application, but you don't want to explicitly manage its life cycle. To make sure you have some data to work with, whenever you use weak references, you should also add instrumentation/logic to ensure that your weak reference strategy is working. At a minimum, track how often you need to recreate the data and how much time you are spending recreating it.

We can initialize a weak reference with code similar to that in Listing 6.5.

```
private WeakReference _weak;
public  void Initialize(string xmlPath)
{
  XmlDocument document = new XmlDocument();
  document.Load(xmlPath);
  _weak = new WeakReference(document);
}
```

**Listing 6.5:**   Initializing a weak reference.

After the `Initialize` method, there are no strong references to the XML document that we loaded; the only reference is the weak reference in the `_weak` variable. If, after we call the `Initialize` method, the GC runs, then the weak reference will be collected and we will have no access to the document. If the GC does not run, then the original document will still be accessible in the `WeakReference` variable.

We can interrogate and use the weak reference with code similar to that shown in Listing 6.6.

```
public void Parse ()
{
  XmlDocument document = null;
  if ( _weak.IsAlive )
     document = _weak.Target as XmlDocument;
  if (document == null)
  {
     // log that weak reference was lost
     // recreate the document
  }
  // handle the parsing
}
```

**Listing 6.6:**   Testing to see if the weak reference is still valid.

If you find that you have to recreate the object frequently, or if your original estimate for how much time it takes to recreate the data is inaccurate, you may want to revisit the choice to use weak references. In almost all cases, you will be better served with reviewing your instrumentation data periodically to ensure that you are still getting the results that you expect. If you don't get the results you expect, you will almost certainly simplify your application logic by removing the weak reference logic.

# Marshaling

Occasionally you may need to access functionality that is exposed in a native DLL. This is not common, because the CLR is quite extensive, but it is a good idea to understand what happens behind the scenes. Also if you use .NET Reflector to browse the source code for the framework, you will find this crop up from time to time, and you need to know what is going on.

Marshaling can definitely have a memory impact. The MSDN documentation makes it clear when it states that the `Marshal` class "*provides a collection of methods for allocating unmanaged memory, copying unmanaged memory blocks, and converting managed to unmanaged types, as well as other miscellaneous methods used when interacting with unmanaged code."* (see HTTP://MSDN.MICROSOFT.COM/EN-US/LIBRARY/ SYSTEM.RUNTIME.INTEROPSERVICES.MARSHAL.ASPX).

Unmanaged memory means no GC which, in turn, means that anything that you allocate, you must also explicitly de-allocate. When you start working with unmanaged memory, you are explicitly going out on a limb and leaving the safety net that .NET provides. Naturally, this is not for the faint of heart, and any code that uses these techniques must be carefully monitored, not just for memory leaks but also for type safety.

Some data types are interoperable and will work the same in an unmanaged world as they do in the managed world, while others do not, and will need to be explicitly converted. The basic integral types are interoperable, and pointers are at least interoperable in unsafe mode. It may be surprising to find out that some other common types, such as `Char`, are not interoperable. In managed code, a char will be a 2-byte Unicode character, but in unmanaged code it will be a 1-byte ASCII character. `Bool` is another tricky type; in unmanaged code, a `bool` is typically an integral value with 0 meaning `false` and anything else being `true`. Any integer value can server in the place of a `bool`. For instance, the code in Listings 6.7 and 6.8 is valid in C++, but not in C#.

```
int x = list.Count;
if (x)  // Invalid in C#
{
    Console.WriteLine("The list is not empty.");
}
```

**Listing 6.7:** Booleans are treated differently in C++.

```
int x = list.Count;
if (x > 0)  // Valid in C#
{
    Console.WriteLine("The list is not empty.");
}
```

**Listing 6.8:** Integers are not booleans in C#.

When you call unmanaged methods that expect or return a `bool`, you should use `int` instead, and when you call unmanaged methods that expect or return a pointer (\*), you should use `IntPtr` instead. This will limit the scope of "unsafe" operations.

Interoperability issues aside, there are potentially significant memory issues to pay attention to. It is common to have to allocate unmanaged memory to be referenced and manipulated by the target of your DLL call. Naturally, this unmanaged memory is outside the oversight of the GC, and so it is up to the humble developer to limit its scope and ensure that the memory is released appropriately.

This sounds like a great place for the disposable pattern that we have previously discussed but, without some clever reworking on your part, this will not work as expected. For starters, there is no single object that would need to implement the `IDisposable` interface. We don't need to dispose of the `Marshal` class, but rather the memory allocated by this class. While you could create a memory wrapper and have it host the allocated memory and implement the `IDisposable` interface, you can also easily revert to a basic try-catch-finally block, as shown in Listing 6.9.

```
var size = 32*Marshal.SizeOf(new byte());
var allocatedMemory = IntPtr.Zero;
var stringPointer = IntPtr.Zero;
try
{
    allocatedMemory = Marshal.AllocHGlobal(size);
    stringPointer =
    Marshal.StringToHGlobalAnsi(stringValue);
    // Make your dll method calls
}
catch
{
    // log the exception as needed
    throw;
}
finally
{
    if (allocatedMemory != IntPtr.Zero)
    Marshal.FreeHGlobal(allocatedMemory);
```

```
    if (stringPointer != IntPtr.Zero )
    Marshal.FreeHGlobal(stringPointer );
}
```

**Listing 6.9:** Explicitly free unmanaged memory that has been allocated.

In this example, you would effectively leak 32 bytes of data every time this method is called, in addition to however many bytes were needed to hold the `stringValue`. This could easily become a memory flood instead of just a leak.

As a rule, I'd recommend that you isolate code that allocates or uses marshaled memory to a central location. This type of logic should not be spread throughout your code base, but rather isolated to proxy classes providing access to the desired unmanaged functionality. Additionally, this code should be routinely monitored to ensure that all best practices are consistently followed, because these code constructs are easily abused.

# Conclusion

The world of software advances at an amazing pace. Fortunately for us, the .NET framework advances at an equally amazing pace. As hardware advancements have made 64-bit architectures more prevalent, the framework kept pace, to provide excellent support for 64-bit programs. Future versions will assuredly continue to keep pace, providing ever-improving support for parallel and asynchronous programming to take advantage of similar hardware advances in multicore technology.

The GC is a pillar of the .NET framework, separating it from all other development platforms; indeed the success of the framework is *directly* tied to how effective the GC is. The GC's effectiveness is at least partly a function of how well it stays out of the way of developers, and avoids being overtly noticed by the user. Each new version of .NET has set out to make the GC less and less intrusive, yet more effective at managing memory – a powerful combination.

As a general rule, use Workstation GC for any program that the user will interact with directly. If you are running a server process, obviously you should use Server GC. Always test your application and configuration under the expected load to ensure that you have the optimal configuration. And remember: conventional wisdom may not always hold true.

Because the GC has gotten so good at staying out of our way, it is easy to forget that it is there, and easy to forget all that it is doing for us. This makes it even easier to get into trouble when we venture into areas such as marshaling, where we explicitly bypass it. Any code relying on marshaling should be consolidated to a single location, making it easier to monitor. Such code should be carefully reviewed to make sure that it continues to be well behaved.

If you stay mindful of the impact your code has on the GC, and the impact the GC has on your code's performance, then you'll find your applications will always be the better for it.

# Chapter 7: The Windows Memory Model

In Chapter 3, we touched on how the .NET CLR interfaces with the Windows OS during heap management. Well, seeing as this is the last chapter and you've come this far, I was hoping maybe you would be willing to go a little bit deeper into the OS.

To really understand memory management, you need to follow what actually happens after the .NET CLR makes memory requests to the OS as part of creating and destroying the generational segments.

As always, let's start with the basics and build from there, "assuming nothing." Of course, you can always skip the first few sections if you find them too basic.

## .NET/OS Interaction

The .NET CLR interfaces with the OS using the Windows API. To control heap management, it creates and drops segments for each generation using specific API calls.

The key APIs are:

- `VirtualAlloc` – allocate virtual memory
- `VirtualFree` – free allocated memory.

`VirtualAlloc` is a key function because it allows .NET to reserve portions of the virtual memory address space in chunks, for use in the creation of segments when they are needed. However, only when the memory is actually required does .NET claim the reserved virtual memory.

It is important to remember that the allocated memory is virtual, which means it doesn't directly refer to physical memory. Instead, it refers to a virtual memory address that is translated by the CPU to a physical memory address on demand.

The reason for using virtual addresses is to allow for a much more flexible memory space to be constructed; one which is far larger than what is actually available in physical RAM. To make this possible, a machine's hard drive is used as a kind of secondary memory store to increase the total amount of memory available to our applications, and we will now explore that virtual/physical relationship.

# Virtual and Physical Memory

Physical memory is simply the amount of physical RAM installed on the machine. By definition, it has a fixed size that can only be increased by opening the back of the machine and slotting more inside.

Any resource with a fixed limit causes a problem; once that limit is reached – bang – there is nowhere to go. In the absence of any other kind of memory, once the physical memory is all used up, things start to go horribly wrong.

Virtual memory was devised as a way around the problem: using a machine's hard drive as a kind of alternative memory store of last resort. Physical disk capacity is much greater than RAM capacity, and so it makes sense to use part of your disk storage as a way of increasing the amount of available memory. To facilitate this, a large file is created, often called a "swap" or "page" file, which is used to store physical memory sections that haven't been accessed for a while. This allows the memory manager (MM) to reuse physical memory and still have access to "paged" data when requested. I probably don't need to mention the downside of this cunning solution, but I will, anyway: **accessing bits from RAM is pretty fast; getting them off a disk is really slow.**

Virtual memory uses a combination of physical, RAM-based memory and disk-based memory to create a uniform virtual memory address space. Combining the two resources into a single pool gives applications access to a far larger and, as far as processes are concerned, homogenous memory space. In Figure 7.1 you can see a Virtual Address Space (VAS) made up of a sequence of memory blocks, or pages, which point to either physical or disk-based memory.

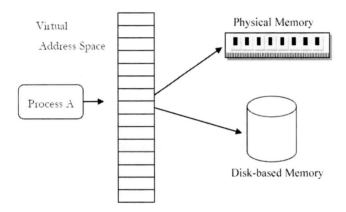

**Figure 7.1:**    Process Virtual Address Space.

# Pages

The virtual memory address space is organized into chunks, or pages, and there are two types of pages (you can specify page size in `VirtualAlloc`):

- small (4 KB)

- large (16 MB).

When a chunk of memory is requested by the .NET runtime, a set of virtual pages, sufficiently large to accommodate the requested size, are allocated. If you asked for 9 K, you would get three pages at 4 K each, that is, 12 K in total.

# The process address space

Figure 7.1 illustrates how process A has access to its own Virtual Address Space (VAS). When process A reads an address from the VAS, that address's actual location, be it in physical memory or on disk, is determined and then translated to the physical address by the operating system's Virtual Memory Manager (VMM), which takes care of all retrieval and storage of memory, as required. We'll take a closer look at the VMM shortly.

The possible size of the memory space (often called address space) depends on the version of Windows running, and whether it's a 32- or a 64-bit system.

## 32-bit address space

Each 32-bit Windows OS process has a maximum address space of 4 GB, which is calculated as $2^{32}$. This is split between a private space of 2 GB for each process, and a space of 2 GB for the OS's dedicated use, and for any shared use (things like DLLs, which use up address space in the process, but aren't counted in the working set or private bytes end up in here; we'll come to this later).

> **Note**
>
> *It is possible for a 32-bit process to access up to 3 GB, if it's compiled as Large Address aware and the OS is booted with the correct option.*

## 64-bit address space

For 64-bit Windows processes, the available address space depends on the processor architecture. It would be *theoretically* possible for a 64-bit system to address up to 18 exabytes (264). However, in reality, current 64-bit processors use 44 bits for addressing virtual memory, allowing for 16 terabytes (TB) of memory, which is equally split between user mode (application processes) and kernel mode (OS processes and drivers). 64-bit Windows applications therefore have a private space of up to 8 TB.

What decides which bits within the VAS are stored on disk or in RAM? The answer is "the memory manager."

# Memory Manager

With the exception of kernel mode processes, which can access memory directly, all other memory addresses are virtual addresses, which means that when a thread accesses memory, the CPU has to determine where the data is actually located. As we know, it can be in one of two places:

- physical memory
- disk (inside a page file).

If the data is already in memory, then the CPU just translates the virtual address to the physical memory address of the data, and access is achieved. On the other hand, if the data is on the disk, then a "page fault" occurs, and the memory manager has to load the data *from* the disk into a physical memory location. Only then can it translate virtual and physical addresses (we'll look at how data is moved back out to pages when we discuss page faults in more detail, later in this chapter).

Now, when a thread needs to allocate a memory page (see the *Pages* section, above), it makes a request to the MM, which allocates virtual pages (using `VirtualAlloc`) and also manages when the physical memory pages are actually created.

To free up memory, the MM just frees the physical and disk-based memory, and marks the virtual address range as free.

Processes and developers are completely unaware of what's going on under the hood. Their memory accesses just work, even though they have been translated, and may first have been loaded from disk.

# Using the memory manager

As mentioned earlier, when you request memory using `VirtualAlloc`, the entire process is mediated by the memory manager, and you have three choices available to you. You can:

- **reserve** the virtual memory address range for future use (fast, and ensures the memory will be available, but requires a later commit)

- **claim** it immediately (slower, as physical space has to be found and allocated)

- **commit** previously reserved memory.

Claiming your memory immediately is called "committing," and means that whatever you have committed will be allocated in the page file, but will only make it into physical RAM memory when first used. On the other hand, "reserving" just means that the memory is available for use at some point in the future, but isn't yet associated with any physical storage. Later on, you can commit portions of the reserved virtual memory, but reserving it first is a faster process in the short term, and means that the necessary memory is definitely available to use when you commit it later on (not to mention faster to commit).

# Keeping track

To keep track of what has been allocated in a process's VAS, the memory manager maintains a structure called the **Virtual Address Descriptor (VAD)** tree.

Each VAD entry in the tree contains data about the virtual allocation including:

- start address

- end address

- committed size (0 if reserved)

- protection info (Read, Write, etc.), which is actually outside the scope of this book.

If you look at the parameters of `VirtualAlloc` on the Microsoft developer network at HTTP://TINYURL.COM/VIRTUALALLOC, you can see how some of its parameters are used to build the VAD.

```
LPVOID WINAPI VirtualAlloc(
    __in_opt  LPVOID lpAddress,
    __in      SIZE_T dwSize,
    __in      DWORD flAllocationType,
    __in      DWORD flProtect);
```

**Listing 7.1:** `VirtualAlloc` function prototype.

`VirtualAlloc` (Listing 7.1) takes the following parameters:

- `lpAddress` – virtual address

- size of allocation

- `flAllocationType` includes values:

  - `MEM_COMMIT`

  - `MEM_RESERVE`

- `flProtect` includes values:

  - `PAGE_READWRITE`

  - `PAGE_READ`.

So, the VAS state is entirely held within the VAD tree, and this is the starting point for virtual memory management. Any attempt to access virtual memory (read or write) is first checked to ensure access is being made to an existing virtual address, and only then is an attempt made to translate addresses.

# Page Frame Database

So far, we've talked about tracking virtual memory. The next piece of the puzzle is physical memory; specifically, how does the memory manager know which physical memory pages are free/used/corrupt, and so on?

The answer is the **Page Frame Database** (**PFD**), which contains a representation of each page in physical memory. A page can be in one of a number of states, including:

- `Valid` – in use

- `Free` – available for use, but still contains data and needs zeroing before use

- `Zeroed` – ready for allocation.

As you can probably guess, the PFD is heavily used by the VMM.

So far we know that the memory manager uses:

- the VAD to keep track of virtual memory

- the PFD to keep track of physical memory.

*But*, as yet there is no way of translating between virtual addresses and physical memory! To do that, another mapping structure is required, called the **page table**, which maps virtual pages to their actual locations in memory and on disk.

# The Page Table

Once a page has been committed using `VirtualAlloc`, it's only when it's accessed for the first time that anything actually happens. When a thread accesses the committed virtual memory, physical RAM memory is allocated and the corresponding virtual and physical addresses are recorded as an entry in a new structure called the **page table** (see Figure 7.2).

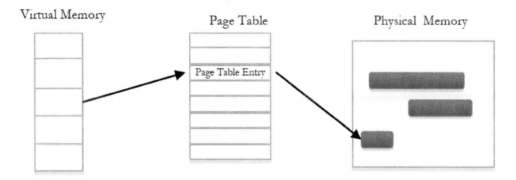

**Figure 7.2:** Conceptual page table design.

So the page table stores the physical memory address and its corresponding virtual address, and is key to address translation.

Each page table entry records when the page was changed and if it's still loaded in physical memory.

Committed pages are backed up to the page file on disk. When a page hasn't been used for a while, the memory manager determines if it can be removed from physical memory. When this removal or unused pages happen, the MM just leaves a copy on disk in the page file.

Using a set of complex algorithms, the VMM can swap pages in and out of memory based on their usage patterns and demand. This gives applications access to a large memory space, protected memory, and efficient use of memory, all at the same time.

We will look at page swapping in more detail later on, but let's now look a little deeper into address translation.

# Virtual Addresses and the Page Table

Having one huge page table describing every page for the entire memory space would be a very inefficient structure to search when looking for a page.

So, to optimize things, instead of having one large page table, the information is split into multiple page tables, and an index is used to direct the memory manager to the appropriate one for any given request. This index is called the **directory index**.

To translate a 32-bit virtual address into a physical address, it is first split up into three parts:

- directory index (first 10 bits)

- page index (next 10 bits)

- byte offset (last 12 bits).

The three parts of the address are used to navigate through the directory index and the page table to locate the precise address in physical memory.

Figure 7.3 illustrates how the address translation takes place using the three parts of the virtual address.

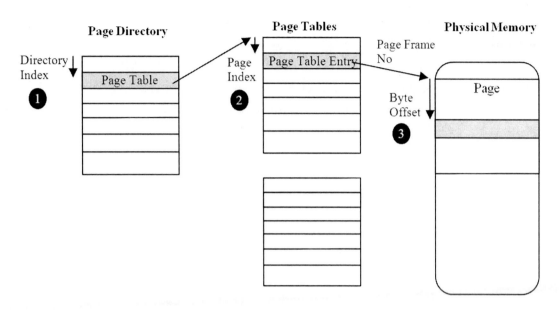

**Figure 7.3:** Page table structure.

When a virtual address is translated, the first 10 bits are used as an index into the process's directory index table (1). The directory index item at this location contains the address of the page table which the system should use for the next lookup, and the next 10 bits of the virtual address are used as an index into this table (2) which gives the page table entry for the virtual page.

The page table entry is what we ultimately need, because it describes the virtual page and whether the actual page is resident in physical memory. If it is, then the physical memory address (page frame number) is used to find the start of the desired memory address along with the last 12 bits of the virtual address. These last 12 bits are used as an offset from the start of the physical address of the page (3) to give the exact location of the requested memory chunk.

We've just translated a virtual to a physical address!

It's worth pointing out that each process has its own page directory index, the address of which is stored in a specific CPU register so as to be always available when a process thread is running.

The mechanisms for 64-bit processes and 32-bit processes with **physical address extensions** (**PAE**) are similar, but both involve more deeply nested table structures to cope with overhead of the larger address space, and the virtual address structure also differs. However, the principle is the same so, in the interests of clarity, I will leave it there.

# Page Table Entry

As you have hopefully deduced from the previous sections, the **page table entry** (**PTE**) is the key piece of information in virtual addressing because it holds the physical memory location of the virtual page. Perhaps even more crucially, it records whether the entry is valid or not. When valid (i.e. the valid bit is set), the page is actually loaded in physical memory. Otherwise (i.e. when invalid) there are one of several possible problems interfering with the addressing process, the least of which will require the page to be reloaded from the page file.

The PTE also stores some info about page security and usage info, but that's another story.

# Page Faults

When access is attempted to a virtual page with a PTE validity bit set to zero, it's called a page fault. The requested page isn't in physical memory, so something else is going to have to happen.

If all is well, then the missing page should be in the page file, and its location stored within the PTE. In that case, it's just a simple matter of loading the page from the page file and allocating it to a page frame in physical memory.

Another example might be the first time a reserved address is accessed; in this situation, there's naturally no physical memory associated with it, and so a page fault occurs. The OS responds to this by allocating a new empty page which, in most cases, doesn't involve reading anything from disk.

With plenty of free space available, the solutions to both of these situations are easy jobs. However, it's more difficult under low memory conditions, when the memory manager has to choose a resident page to remove in order to make space.

To do this, Windows looks at physical pages from all user processes to determine the best candidates to be replaced. Pages which are selected for replacement are written to the page file and then overwritten with the requested page data. Each of the PTEs are then adjusted, and address translation completes with the correct page in memory.

When discussing data being moved between physical memory and page files, it's worth talking about a process's **working set**, which is the set of its pages currently resident in physical memory, not counting any shared resources like DLLs. Windows Task Manager shows memory usage in terms of **working set**, which means that when a process's pages are swapped out to disk, its working set goes down, but its allocated virtual memory is not decreasing, which can lead to confusion.

# Locking Memory

If processes need to stop their pages from being replaced, they can lock them in memory by calling the `VirtualAlloc` API. This should a familiar notion, as we discussed object pinning in Chapter 3, and that is all about locking memory. Regardless, it's usually best to leave it to the OS to decide its own page replacement policy.

# Putting It All Together

We've covered a lot of pretty dense concepts in this chapter, so let's just recap on what happens when a memory address is accessed by a process.

Figure 7.4 illustrates what happens when a process requests a virtual memory address.

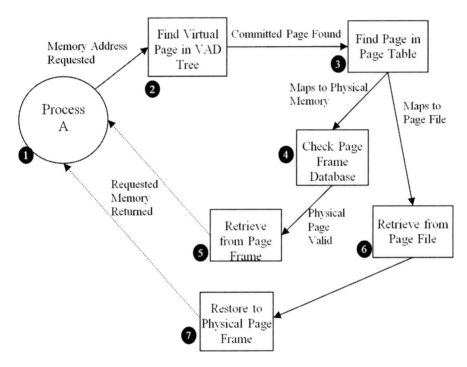

**Figure 7.4:** Mapping a virtual address.

When a process requests to read a virtual memory address the steps below occur.

1.  Process A requests a virtual memory address.

2.  The VAD tree is checked to ensure the address falls within a valid committed virtual page. If not, an exception is thrown.

3. The virtual address is broken down into its constituent parts and used to find the PTE in the page table.

4. If the PTE thinks the page is in physical memory, then the page frame entry is retrieved from the PFD.

5. It is checked for validity, and used to retrieve the actual data from the direct location in physical memory, which is then returned to process A.

6. If the page isn't in physical memory, then a page fault occurs and it has to be loaded in from the page file. An existing physical page may have to be replaced to achieve this.

7. Once restored, the requested memory can be returned from physical memory.

It really is that simple!

OK, that was a joke. The truth is that it *is* a bit convoluted and complicated, but if you had designed a system to achieve something similar, you would probably have used many of the same structures and processes.

# Memory Caching

So as not to confuse you with information overload, I have deliberately left out the role of the processor memory caches in all of this.

Basically, the contents of the most frequently accessed memory addresses will be stored on the CPU itself (or just off) inside a multilevel data cache, the purpose being to speed up memory access with fast memory hardware and shorter access paths.

The data cache is split into three levels called L1, L2 and L3. The L1 and L2 caches are on the CPU, with L1 allowing for the fastest access, and typically storing between 8 and 64 KB. The L2 cache store is larger than the L1 cache (typically up to 2 MB), but access is slower.

The L3 cache is stored on the motherboard and is the largest cache store; for example, the Intel Core I7 processor has an 8 MB L3 cache. It's the slowest of all three caches, but still faster than direct memory access.

When a memory address is requested, the caches are checked first, before an attempt is made to access physical RAM, and the OS only actually has to deal with the paging file at the end of that checking sequence.

The access order is L1->L2->L3->physical memory->page file.

The intricacies of the data cache could fill a whole new chapter in themselves, but we'll not go there in this book, as I think we've covered enough for now.

# The Long and Winding Road

We've gone from an allocation and garbage collection in .NET, right through object retention and promotion, and on to subsequent allocation of ephemeral segments. Beyond segments, we looked at how `VirtualAlloc` is used to create ephemeral segments, what `VirtualAlloc` actually does, and what it translates to. Finally, we've broken memory allocation down into its raw representation within the OS, and analyzed how huge Virtual Address Spaces are managed to give processes access to resources far in excess of their machine's physical memory limitations.

# Summary

Maybe you're wondering why you needed to know all this. Well, I suppose the short answer is because what happens beyond the .NET boundary is no longer a mystery. .NET is built on top of the Windows API, and so its impacts and limitations come from there as well.

There will be a knock-on effect from understanding lower-level memory, not least from when you are using performance counters to analyze performance of a server. Many of the metrics available should now make a lot more sense and, taken in concert with how .NET itself is behaving, will now better complement each other to give you a much fuller picture of the system's behavior.

Stopping your education at the .NET level always leaves you open to that uncertainty about "what happens from this point?" Don't get me wrong, abstractions are incredibly useful and, when the systems we're working with are as complex as this, absolutely necessary. But it doesn't hurt to have a deeper understanding.

If you started this book with little or no knowledge of .NET memory management and you've made it this far, then you've finished with a pretty comprehensive understanding of the whole subject. And make no mistake, that's a good thing, because what you do in code will affect how these systems behave, which will determine how your application performs. Understanding what goes on under the hood may change for ever how you write your code.

# Index

## Symbols

# .NET and
# SQL Server Tools
## from Red Gate Software

Pricing and information about Red Gate tools are correct at the time of
going to print. For the latest information and pricing on all Red Gate's
tools, visit www.red-gate.com

ingeniously simple tools

# ANTS Memory Profiler

$495

Find memory leaks and optimize memory usage

↗ Find memory leaks within minutes

↗ Jump straight to the heart of the problem with intelligent summary information, filtering options and visualizations

↗ Optimize the memory usage of your C# and VB.NET code

> **"Freaking sweet! We have a known memory leak that took me about four hours to find using our current tool, so I fired up ANTS Memory Profiler and went at it like I didn't know the leak existed. Not only did I come to the conclusion much faster, but I found another one!"**
>
> **Aaron Smith** IT Manager, R.C. Systems Inc.

# ANTS Performance Profiler

from **$395**

Profile your .NET code and boost the performance of your application

↗ Identify performance bottlenecks within minutes

↗ Drill down to slow lines of code thanks to line-level code timings

↗ Boost the performance of your .NET code

↗ Get the most complete picture of your application's performance with integrated SQL and File I/O profiling

> **"ANTS Performance Profiler took us straight to the specific areas of our code which were the cause of our performance issues."**
>
> **Terry Phillips** Sr Developer,
> Harley-Davidson Dealer Systems

> **"Thanks to ANTS Performance Profiler, we were able to discover a performance hit in our serialization of XML that was fixed for a 10x performance increase."**
>
> **Garret Spargo** Product Manager, AFHCAN

Visit **www.red-gate.com** for a 14-day, free trial

## .NET Reflector®

### from $35

Decompile, browse, analyse and debug .NET code

↗ View, navigate and search through the class hierarchies of any .NET assembly, even if you don't have access to the source code

↗ Decompile and analyse any .NET assembly in C#, Visual Basic and IL

↗ Step straight into decompiled assemblies whilst debugging in Visual Studio, with the same debugging techniques you would use on your own code

"One of the most useful, practical debugging tools that I have ever worked with in .NET! It provides complete browsing and debugging features for .NET assemblies, and has clean integration with Visual Studio."
**Tom Baker** Consultant Software Engineer, EMC Corporation

"EVERY DEVELOPER NEEDS THIS TOOL!"
**Daniel Larson** Software Architect, NewsGator Technologies

## SmartAssembly®

### from $795

.NET obfuscation, automated error reporting and feature usage reporting

↗ **Obfuscation:** Obfuscate your .NET code and protect your IP

↗ **Automated Error Reporting:** Get quick and automatic reports on exceptions your end-users encounter and identify unforeseen bugs within hours or days of shipping. Receive detailed reports containing a stack trace and values of the local variables, making debugging easier

↗ **Feature Usage Reporting:** Get insight into how your customers are using your application, rely on hard data to plan future development, and enhance your users' experience with your software

"Knowing the frequency of problems (especially immediately after a release) is extremely helpful in prioritizing and triaging bugs that are reported internally. Additionally, by having the context of where those errors occurred, including debugging information, really gives you that leap forward to start troubleshooting and diagnosing the issue."
**Ed Blankenship** Technical Lead and MVP

Visit **www.red-gate.com** for a 14-day, free trial

# SQL Compare® Pro $595

Compare and synchronize SQL Server database schemas

↗ Eliminate mistakes migrating database changes from dev, to test, to production

↗ Speed up the deployment of new database schema updates

↗ Find and fix errors caused by differences between databases

↗ Compare and synchronize within SSMS

> "Just purchased SQL Compare. With the productivity I'll get out of this tool, it's like buying time."
>
> **Robert Sondles** Blueberry Island Media Ltd

# SQL Data Compare Pro $595

Compares and synchronizes SQL Server database contents

↗ Save time by automatically comparing and synchronizing your data

↗ Copy lookup data from development databases to staging or production

↗ Quickly fix problems by restoring damaged or missing data to a single row

↗ Compare and synchronize data within SSMS

> "We use SQL Data Compare daily and it has become an indispensable part of delivering our service to our customers. It has also streamlined our daily update process and cut back literally a good solid hour per day."
>
> **George Pantela** GPAnalysis.com

Visit **www.red-gate.com** for a 14-day, free trial

# SQL Prompt Pro                                        $295

Write, edit, and explore SQL effortlessly

- ↗ Write SQL smoothly, with code-completion and SQL snippets
- ↗ Reformat SQL to a preferred style
- ↗ Keep databases tidy by finding invalid objects automatically
- ↗ Save time and effort with script summaries, smart object renaming and more

> **"SQL Prompt is hands-down one of the coolest applications I've used. Makes querying/developing so much easier and faster."**
> **Jorge Segarra** University Community Hospital

# SQL Source Control                                     $295

Connect your existing source control system to SQL Server

- ↗ Bring all the benefits of source control to your database
- ↗ Source control schemas and data within SSMS, not with offline scripts
- ↗ Connect your databases to TFS, SVN, SourceGear Vault, Vault Pro, Mercurial, Perforce, Git, Bazaar, and any source control system with a capable command line
- ↗ Work with shared development databases, or individual copies
- ↗ Track changes to follow who changed what, when, and why
- ↗ Keep teams in sync with easy access to the latest database version
- ↗ View database development history for easy retrieval of specific versions

> **"After using SQL Source Control for several months, I wondered how I got by before. Highly recommended, it has paid for itself several times over."**
> **Ben Ashley** Fast Floor

Visit **www.red-gate.com** for a 28-day, free trial

# SQL Monitor
from **$795**

SQL Server performance monitoring and alerting

↗ Intuitive overviews at global, cluster, machine, SQL Server, and database levels for up-to-the-minute performance data

↗ Use SQL Monitor's web UI to keep an eye on server performance in real time on desktop machines and mobile devices

↗ Intelligent SQL Server alerts via email and an alert inbox in the UI, so you know about problems first

↗ Comprehensive historical data, so you can go back in time to identify the source of a problem

↗ Generate reports via the UI or with Red Gate's free SSRS Reporting Pack

↗ View the top 10 expensive queries for an instance or database based on CPU usage, duration, and reads and writes

↗ PagerDuty integration for phone and SMS alerting

↗ Fast, simple installation and administration

> "Being web based, SQL Monitor is readily available to you, wherever you may be on your network. You can check on your servers from almost any location, via most mobile devices that support a web browser."
>
> **Jonathan Allen** Senior DBA, Careers South West Ltd

Visit **www.red-gate.com** for a 14-day, free trial

# SQL Virtual Restore $495

Rapidly mount live, fully functional databases direct from backups

- ↗ Virtually restoring a backup requires significantly less time and space than a regular physical restore
- ↗ Databases mounted with SQL Virtual Restore are fully functional and support both read/write operations
- ↗ SQL Virtual Restore is ACID compliant and gives you access to full, transactionally consistent data, with all objects visible and available
- ↗ Use SQL Virtual Restore to recover objects, verify your backups with DBCC CHECKDB, create a storage-efficient copy of your production database, and more

> **"We find occasions where someone has deleted data accidentally or dropped an index, etc., and with SQL Virtual Restore we can mount last night's backup quickly and easily to get access to the data or the original schema. It even works with all our backups being encrypted. This takes any extra load off our production server. SQL Virtual Restore is a great product."**
>
> **Brent McCraken** Senior Database Administrator/Architect, Kiwibank Limited

# SQL Storage Compress $1,595

Silent data compression to optimize SQL Server storage

- ↗ Reduce the storage footprint of live SQL Server databases by up to 90% to save on space and hardware costs
- ↗ Databases compressed with SQL Storage Compress are fully functional
- ↗ Prevent unauthorized access to your live databases with 256-bit AES encryption
- ↗ Integrates seamlessly with SQL Server and does not require any configuration changes

Visit **www.red-gate.com** for a 14-day, free trial

# SQL Toolbelt

# $1,995

The essential SQL Server tools for database professionals

You can buy our acclaimed SQL Server tools individually or bundled. Our most popular deal is the SQL Toolbelt: fourteen of our SQL Server tools in a single installer, with **a combined value of $5,930 but an actual price of $1,995**, a saving of 66%.

*Fully compatible with SQL Server 2000, 2005, and 2008.*

***SQL Toolbelt contains:***

↗ **SQL Compare Pro**

↗ **SQL Data Compare Pro**

↗ **SQL Source Control**

↗ **SQL Backup Pro**

↗ **SQL Monitor**

↗ **SQL Prompt Pro**

↗ **SQL Data Generator**

↗ **SQL Doc**

↗ **SQL Dependency Tracker**

↗ **SQL Packager**

↗ **SQL Multi Script Unlimited**

↗ **SQL Search**

↗ **SQL Comparison SDK**

↗ **SQL Object Level Recovery Native**

> **"The SQL Toolbelt provides tools that database developers, as well as DBAs, should not live without."**
> **William Van Orden** Senior Database Developer, Lockheed Martin

Visit **www.red-gate.com** for a 14-day, free trial

# Performance Tuning with SQL Server
# Dynamic Management Views
## Louis Davidson and Tim Ford

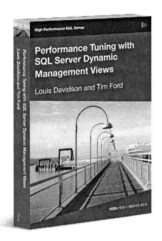

This is the book that will de-mystify the process of using Dynamic Management Views to collect the information you need to troubleshoot SQL Server problems. It will highlight the core techniques and "patterns" that you need to master, and will provide a core set of scripts that you can use and adapt for your own requirements.

ISBN: 978-1-906434-47-2
Published: October 2010

# Defensive Database Programming
## Alex Kuznetsov

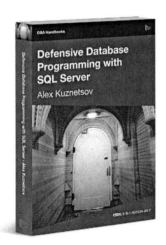

Inside this book, you will find dozens of practical, defensive programming techniques that will improve the quality of your T-SQL code and increase its resilience and robustness.

ISBN: 978-1-906434-49-6
Published: June 2010

# Brad's Sure Guide to
# SQL Server Maintenance Plans
Brad McGehee

Brad's Sure Guide to Maintenance Plans shows you how to use the Maintenance Plan Wizard and Designer to configure and schedule eleven core database maintenance tasks, ranging from integrity checks, to database backups, to index reorganizations and rebuilds.

**ISBN:** 78-1-906434-34-2
**Published:** December 2009

# The Red Gate Guide to SQL Server
# Team-based Development
Phil Factor, Grant Fritchey, Alex Kuznetsov,
and Mladen Prajdić

This book shows how to use a mixture of home-grown scripts, native SQL Server tools, and tools from the Red Gate SQL Toolbelt, to successfully develop database applications in a team environment, and make database development as similar as possible to "normal" development.

**ISBN:** 978-1-906434-59-5
**Published:** November 2010

CPSIA information can be obtained at www.ICGtesting.com
Printed in the USA
BVOW061204080413

317595BV00004B/28/P